Independently published
ISBN: 9783911386166
© G. Conti 2024 & D. Viñales

Edited by Laura García Gracia

Images were produced using Microsoft Copilot, Pixabay, Midjourney or OpenAI
Cover image of Sunset over Port de Alcudia, Majorca, Balearic islands from iStock

A New GCSE Spanish Workbook

Part Two

Gianfranco Conti, Dylan Viñales & Ana del Casar

Edited by Laura García Gracia

A New GCSE Spanish Workbook – PART TWO

This workbook is for students and teachers preparing for the GCSE Spanish exams beginning in 2026 (first teaching September 2024). It is the second of two books covering a total of 10 thematic areas.

Each one of the five units in this book consists of the following:

1. Foundation Tier vocabulary building exercises.
2. Foundation Tier exam-style reading tasks.
3. Higher Tier vocabulary building exercises.
4. Higher Tier exam-style reading tasks.
5. A Grammar Focus section with explanations and practice exercises.
6. Pre-speaking and writing exercises.
7. An exam-style photo task for both tiers.
8. An exam-style role-play task for both tiers.
9. Exam-style writing tasks for both tiers.
10. Two banks of model sentences, one for each tier.

At the end of the workbook, there is a set of answers to the exercises from parts 1-6 above.

We know how important frequent repetition is for students of all levels of proficiency. Therefore, each unit has been carefully planned to recycle the same words, chunks and sentences many times over to help students remember as much as possible when they do the exam. In addition, many high-frequency vocabulary items and grammatical structures are encountered across all the units.

The content has been written to take account of the DfE's requirement that GCSE students become familiar with aspects of the contexts and cultures in which Spanish is spoken. The comprehension texts were written by the authors, often drawing on authentic sources.

Thematic, vocabulary and grammar content has been matched against the new specifications and should be suitable for both AQA and Pearson-Edexcel. We have stuck very closely indeed to the word lists provided by the awarding bodies.

How to use the book

Students may work through the whole book, or teachers may like to photocopy individual pages, sections or whole units. Teachers or students can use the answers provided for checking or marking.

Acknowledgments

Our heartfelt thanks to our superb team of Guest Proofreaders who kindly assisted with the proofing of the text: **Catalina Petre, Hannah Foote, Barry Agnew, Ana Amores Márquez, Victoria Harrison, Sonja Fedrizzi & Ryan Cockrell.**

Gianfranco, Dylan & Ana

Contents
Part Two

UNIT 1

Relationships and identity

Contents

- Foundation vocab building
- Foundation reading
- Higher vocab building
- Higher reading
- Grammar focus: adjectives
- Preparing for speaking and writing
- Writing and speaking from a photo card
- Speaking in a role play
- Writing
- Sentence banks

Unit 1 - Foundation vocab building

Vocabulary

agradable	*pleasant*
alemán/a	*German*
amable	*kind*
bonito/a	*beautiful*
caer/caerse	*to fall*
la cara	*face*
el chico/a	*boy, girl*
conocer	*to know, get to know*
corto/a	*short (object, not person)*
discutir	*to argue*
divorciarse	*to get divorced*
la edad	*age*
egoísta	*selfish*
enamorarse de	*to fall in love with*
enfadarse	*to get angry*
entender	*to understand*
el familiar	*relative*
fatal	*awful*
gracioso/a	*funny*
grande	*big*
guapo/a	*good-looking*
hablador/a	*talkative*
el hijo/a	*son, daughter*
horrible	*horrible*
el idioma	*language*
igual	*equal*
joven	*young*
la juventud	*youth*
llevarse bien	*to get on well*
la madrastra	*step-mother*
el marido	*husband*
el matrimonio	*marriage*
morir	*to die*
muerto/a	*dead*
la mujer	*woman, wife*
el niño/a	*child*
la novia	*girlfriend/bride*
el novio	*boyfriend/groom*
el padrastro	*stepfather*
pasar	*to spend (time)*
preocupado/a	*worried*
separarse	*to separate*
simpático/a	*nice*
solo/a	*alone*
soltero/a	*single*
el tamaño	*size*
trabajador/a	*hard-working*
triste	*sad*
la unión civil	*civil partnership*
vago/a	*lazy*
la vida	*life*
viejo/a	*old (mostly objects)*
vivir	*to live*

1. Match up.

Simpático	Worried
Soltero	Single
Agradable	Young
Triste	Fun
Igual	Equal
Hablador	Sad
Divertido	Old
Preocupado	Talkative
Joven	Pleasant
Viejo	Nice

2. Broken words.

a. No_ _ _: *Boyfriend*

b. Co_ _ _: *Short (m)*

c. Ni_ _: *Child (m)*

d. Gra_ _ _ _ _: *Funny (m)*

e. Eg_ _ _ _ a: *Selfish*

f. Jo_ _ _: *Young*

g. Vi_ _ _: *Old (m)*

h. No_ _ _: *Girlfriend*

i. Ma_ _ _ _: *Husband*

3. Gapped translation.

a. Él se enfada: *He gets __________.*

b. Mi mujer tiene 40 años: *My __________ is 40 years old.*

c. Yo tengo un hijo y una hija: *I have a _______ and a ________.*

d. Yo estoy un poco preocupado: *I am a bit _________.*

e. Ella está soltera: *She is _________.*

f. Su marido ha muerto: *Her ________ has died.*

g. Su hermana es más joven: *His ________ is younger.*

4. Faulty translation: spot and correct the wrong translations.

a. Ella tiene el pelo corto: *She has long hair.*

b. Me llevo mal con mis padres: *I get on well with my parents.*

c. Mi padre está feliz: *My father is worried.*

d. Él es un poco mayor: *He is a bit young.*

e. Me llevo bien con mi padrastro: *I get on with my father.*

f. Me enfado a menudo con ellos: *I often spend time with them.*

5. Complete the words in each of the categories below.

a. Adjectives (appearance): g________, j________, v__________

b. Adjectives (personality): g________, v________, s__________

c. Family members: p__________, m__________, n__________

6. Translate into English.

a. Caerse: __________   f. Morir: __________

b. Enfadarse: __________   g. Vago: __________

c. Solo: __________   h. Vivir: __________

d. Soltero: __________   i. Simpático: __________

e. Hablador: __________   j. Pasar: __________

7. Complete the sentences.

a. Mi padre es muy t_ _ _ _ _ _ _ _ _.   *My father is very hard-working.*

b. Me l_ _ _ _ bien con él.   *I get on well with him.*

c. Vivo con mi madre y mi h_ _ _ _ _ _.   *I live with my mother and my brother.*

d. D_ _ _ _ _ _ a menudo con mis padres.   *I argue often with my parents.*

e. Ella se e_ _ _ _ _ _ todos los días.   *She falls in love every day.*

f. Ella tiene una cara b_ _ _ _ _.   *She has a beautiful face.*

g. Su m_ _ _ _ _ _ _ _ _ ha sido muy feliz.   *Their marriage has been very happy.*

h. Mis padres son bastante j_ _ _ _ _ _.   *My parents are quite young.*

i. Mi m_ _ _ _ _ _ _ _ es muy amable.   *My stepmother is very kind.*

8. Add in the missing letters.

a. _oven — *young*

b. _aerse — *to fall*

c. _ago/a — *lazy*

d. _ivertido/a — *funny*

e. _oltero/a — *single*

f. _ida — *life*

g. _atal — *awful*

h. _ovio — *boyfriend*

9. Multiple choice: circle the right option.

a. Muerto	Happy	Dead	Alive
b. Viejo	Young	Kind	Old
c. Simpático	Sad	Simple	Nice
d. Corto	Short	Long	Cold
e. Bonito	Jolly	Kind	Beautiful
f. Triste	Happy	Sad	Nice
g. Joven	Old	Young	Gentle
h. Amable	Gentle	Unkind	Kind
i. Solo	Alone	Sad	Silly
j. Vago	Kind	Lazy	Nice
k. Trabajador	Lazy	Hard-working	Short

10. Mystery word challenge.

a. Opposite of "feliz": t_____________

b. Not boring: gra_______________

c. Opposite of great: f_____________

d. Opposite of "vivir": m_____________

e. Opposite of "llevarse bien": d_______

f. Mi madre y mi padre: mis p_________

g. La hija de mi hermana: mi s_________

h. Opposite of "largo": c_____________

i. Opposite of "perezoso": t_________

j. Opposite of "casarse": d___________

11. Break the flow and translate: mark the gaps and translate.

e.g. Mi/tío/es/alemán: My uncle is German.

a. Mistíossonamables:

b. Mispadressonjóvenes:

c. Yomellevobienconmispadres:

d. Yodiscutoconmihermano:

e. Mipadreesestricto:

f. Mihermanaestrabajadora:

g. Mipadreessimpático:

h. Eshorrible:

12. Spot and correct the spelling mistakes.

a. Javen (young):

b. Viello (old):

c. Parastro (stepfather):

d. Fatall (awful):

e. Murir (to die):

f. Dibertido (fun):

g. Bonnito (beautiful):

h. Bago (lazy):

13. Unjumble the words.

a. agvo: _________________ (lazy)

b. nojve: _______________ (young)

c. atol: __________________ (tall)

d. nobtoi: ___________ (beautiful)

e. arimdo: ___________ (husband)

f. jmure: _______________ (wife)

g. aaembl: ______________ (kind)

14. Translate into English.

a. Yo vivo con mi madrastra:

b. Yo me llevo bien con mis padres:

c. Mis padres me entienden:

d. Mi hermana es graciosa y amable:

e. Mi padre es trabajador:

f. Mi madre está preocupada:

g. Mi hermano pequeño está triste:

Unit 1 - Foundation reading

1. Read what these young people say about their families.

Marcos
Me llevo muy bien con mis hermanos y hermanas, sobre todo con mi hermano Abel. Es callado y tímido.

Cristina
Somos cuatro en nuestra familia: mis padres, mi hermana y yo. Vivimos juntos en Valencia desde hace cinco años.

Fátima
Vivo con mi madre en un piso. Ella es divertida e inteligente. Hacemos muchas cosas juntas.

Sandra
Mis padres se llaman Juan y María. A veces discuten, pero son muy felices juntos.

Jaime
Me llevo bien con mi hermanastro Samuel. Es un poco molesto, pero en general es simpático.

Who said...?

a. Their family does lots of things together.   ______________
b. Their stepbrother is a bit annoying.   ______________
c. They get on with their brothers and sisters.   ______________
d. Their parents argue sometimes.   ______________
e. Their family has lived together in the same city for five years.   ______________

2. Three young people talk about their friends. Complete the sentences below.

Juan
Creo que es importante tener amigos con personalidades diferentes. Por ejemplo, yo me llevo bien con gente muy tímida y con gente divertida.

Carlos
Mi mejor amigo es Daniel. Nos llevamos bien porque nos gustan las mismas aficiones, sobre todo el deporte.

Cecilia
Paso mucho tiempo con mi mejor amiga, Laura. Nos llevamos bien y hablamos de todo.

a. Who likes to have friends with different personalities?   ________________

b. Who talks about everything with their friend?   ________________

c. Who shares the same interests as their friend?   ________________

Unit 1 - Foundation reading

3. Read what Miriam says about her family.

> Nací en Guinea Ecuatorial, en África. Vine a vivir con mis padres a Sevilla hace cinco años. Luego mis padres se separaron. Al principio fue difícil, pero ahora vivo en un piso pequeño con mi madre y todo va bien. Además, mi madre ha encontrado un nuevo novio que es muy amable. Se llama Gerardo y trabaja en una panadería cerca de casa. Vive en su propio piso.
>
> Por último, veo a mi padre todos los fines de semana porque seguimos llevándonos muy bien.

a. When did Miriam move to Sevilla?

b. Describe where she lives now.

c. How often does she see her father?

d. Who is Gerardo? Mention two points.

4. Víctor writes about his friendships in his home city of Arauco, in Chile. Tick the things he mentions.

> Tengo muchos amigos en mi colegio en Arauco. Jugamos al fútbol juntos en el colegio, hablamos sobre las clases y vamos al club de natación los sábados por la mañana. De vez en cuando también vamos a la playa porque aquí, en Arauco, el agua siempre está a una buena temperatura.
>
> En mi opinión, los amigos son tan importantes como la familia para tener una vida feliz. Sin embargo, a veces necesito pasar tiempo solo. Por ejemplo, me gusta escuchar música en mi habitación.

a. He has a lot of friends.

b. He talks about sport with friends.

c. He goes swimming on Saturday mornings.

d. He goes to the beach with his friends.

e. The water is sometimes cold.

f. Friends are less important than family.

g. He does not like being alone.

h. He listens to music.

Unit 1 - Foundation reading

5. Susana talks about her best friend, Beatriz.

Lo que más me gusta de Beatriz es que siempre escucha a los demás, acepta a las personas que son diferentes a ella y se lleva bien con todo el mundo. Al mismo tiempo, protesta contra la intolerancia y la falta de respeto. No soporta a las personas que no respetan las diferencias de cada persona.

Es importante entender que todos tenemos los mismos derechos. Todos somos diferentes, así que no me gusta la gente que no acepta la identidad de los demás.

   a. What does Susana like the most about Beatriz? Mention two points.

      (i) _______________________________   (ii) _______________________________

   b. What kind of people can't Beatriz stand?

      ____

   c. What does Susana say about identity? Mention two points.

      (i) _______________________________   (ii) _______________________________

6. Mario talks about her parents who were born in Bolivia, but now live in Santiago, Chile.

Mis padres llegaron a Santiago en 1995 para trabajar y estar con sus amigos. Los dos son médicos, así que encontraron trabajo muy pronto. Aquí hace mucho frío en invierno, pero les encanta la ciudad y todas las actividades culturales que ofrece.

Lo que más les gusta es que conocen a todo tipo de gente y que, en general, los lugareños aceptan tanto a las personas de fuera como las nuevas ideas. No quieren volver a Bolivia en el futuro.

Complete the gap in each sentence using a word from the box below. There are more words than gaps.

know	open-minded	different	travel
chemists	work	doctors	meet

   a. Mario's parents came to Santiago to _______________________.

   b. They work as _______________________.

   c. They _______________________ all sorts of different people.

   d. They find people from Santiago to be _______________________.

Unit 1 - Higher vocab building

<table>
<tr><td colspan="2">Vocabulary</td></tr>
<tr><td>acosar</td><td>to bully</td></tr>
<tr><td>agradable</td><td>pleasant</td></tr>
<tr><td>amable</td><td>kind</td></tr>
<tr><td>apoyar</td><td>to support</td></tr>
<tr><td>bonito/a</td><td>beautiful</td></tr>
<tr><td>la broma</td><td>joke</td></tr>
<tr><td>casado/a</td><td>married</td></tr>
<tr><td>caer/caerse</td><td>to fall</td></tr>
<tr><td>cercano/a</td><td>close (friend)</td></tr>
<tr><td>la confianza</td><td>trust</td></tr>
<tr><td>conocer</td><td>to know, get to know</td></tr>
<tr><td>cuidar (de)</td><td>to look after</td></tr>
<tr><td>dar igual</td><td>to not matter</td></tr>
<tr><td>discutir</td><td>to argue</td></tr>
<tr><td>divertido/a</td><td>fun</td></tr>
<tr><td>enfadarse</td><td>to get angry</td></tr>
<tr><td>entender</td><td>to understand</td></tr>
<tr><td>feliz</td><td>happy</td></tr>
<tr><td>gracioso/a</td><td>funny</td></tr>
<tr><td>guapo/a</td><td>good-looking</td></tr>
<tr><td>hablador/a</td><td>talkative</td></tr>
<tr><td>el hijo/a</td><td>son, daughter</td></tr>
<tr><td>horrible</td><td>horrible</td></tr>
<tr><td>joven</td><td>young</td></tr>
<tr><td>llevarse bien</td><td>to get on well</td></tr>
<tr><td>mentir</td><td>to lie</td></tr>
<tr><td>malvado/a</td><td>evil</td></tr>
<tr><td>el matrimonio</td><td>marriage</td></tr>
<tr><td>el marido</td><td>husband</td></tr>
<tr><td>mayor</td><td>old (polite)</td></tr>
<tr><td>molestar</td><td>to annoy</td></tr>
<tr><td>morir</td><td>to die</td></tr>
<tr><td>muerto/a</td><td>dead</td></tr>
<tr><td>la mujer</td><td>woman, wife</td></tr>
<tr><td>orgulloso/a</td><td>proud</td></tr>
<tr><td>parecerse a</td><td>to look like</td></tr>
<tr><td>la pareja</td><td>couple</td></tr>
<tr><td>pasar</td><td>to spend (time)</td></tr>
<tr><td>pobre</td><td>poor</td></tr>
<tr><td>preocupado/a</td><td>worried</td></tr>
<tr><td>rico/a</td><td>rich</td></tr>
<tr><td>sensible</td><td>sensitive</td></tr>
<tr><td>sentir/sentirse</td><td>to feel</td></tr>
<tr><td>separarse</td><td>to separate</td></tr>
<tr><td>simpático/a</td><td>nice</td></tr>
<tr><td>solo/a</td><td>alone</td></tr>
<tr><td>soltero/a</td><td>single</td></tr>
<tr><td>el suegro/a</td><td>father/mother-in-law</td></tr>
<tr><td>trabajador/a</td><td>hard-working</td></tr>
<tr><td>transgénero</td><td>transgender</td></tr>
<tr><td>la unión civil</td><td>civil partnership</td></tr>
<tr><td>vago/a</td><td>lazy</td></tr>
<tr><td>la vida</td><td>life</td></tr>
</table>

1. Match up.

Discutir	To die
Hijo	To fall
Mentir	Man
Broma	To lie
Enfadarse	Equal
Apoyar	To argue
Cercano	To know
Caerse	To support
Conocer	Son
Igual	Close
Morir	To get angry
Hombre	Joke

2. Spot and correct the wrong translations.

a. Novio: *Husband*

b. Hablador: *Talkative*

c. Gracioso: *Hard-working*

d. Preocupado: *Worried*

e. Joven: *Old*

f. Enfadado: *Angry*

g. Mujer: *Woman, wife*

h. Fatal: *Great*

i. Marido: *Relative*

j. Vago: *Good-looking*

3. Gapped translation.

a. Me llevo bien con mi hermano: *I ___________ with my brother.*

b. Mi padre es muy gracioso: *My father is very ________________.*

c. Tengo una hija y un hijo: *I have a _________ and a ___________.*

d. Él cuenta un montón de bromas: *He tells a lot of ____________.*

e. Mi suegra es muy estricta: *My ________________ is very strict.*

f. Mi padre nunca se enfada: *My father never gets _____________.*

g. Ellos se separaron el año pasado: *They _____________ last year.*

4. Multiple choice: circle the right option.

a.	**Morir**	*To be born*	*To die*	*To mourn*
b.	**Cuidar**	*To take care*	*To win*	*To worry*
c.	**Parecerse a**	*To look like*	*To die*	*To annoy*
d.	**Trabajador**	*Hard-working*	*Lazy*	*Talkative*
e.	**Soltero**	*Alone*	*Single*	*Equal*
f.	**Vida**	*Victory*	*Life*	*Death*
g.	**Apoyar**	*To argue*	*To send*	*To support*
h.	**Joven**	*Young*	*Old*	*Kind*
i.	**Viejo**	*Young*	*Vicious*	*Old*

5. Complete with the missing words.

a. Yo ___________ mucho tiempo con mi familia.

b. Ella ____________ con sus padres.

c. Su madre es _____________.

d. Él ___________ mucho a su padre.

e. Mis padres van a _____________ pronto.

f. Ellos _____________ mucho por sus hijos.

g. Mis padres son muy ________________.

h. Ella vive _____________ después de su divorcio.

vive
sola
se preocupan
separarse
simpática
trabajadores
paso
se parece

6. Match the opposites.

Triste	Amable
Vago	Muerto
Niño	Soltero
Vivo	Viejo/anciano
Malvado	Antipático
Joven	Trabajador
Simpático	Adulto
Casado	Genial
Horrible	Con pareja
Solo	Feliz

7. Translate into English.

a. Él está triste: ___________

b. Yo apoyo: ___________

c. Estoy sola: ___________

d. Él es joven: ___________

e. Discutir: ___________

f. Enfadarse: ___________

g. Soltero: ___________

h. Separado: ___________

i. Ella es simpática: _________

j. Mi suegra: ___________

k. Me gusta su cara: _________

l. Ella es guapa: ___________

m. Trabajador: ___________

n. Ella está casada: _________

o. Él es mayor: ___________

p. Me da igual: ___________

q. Vivir en pareja: ___________

r. Él está casado: ___________

8. Separate the words in the sentences below with a line.

a. Ellatrabajaenunhospital — *She works in a hospital.*

b. Ellahacenuevosamigos — *She makes new friends.*

c. Élsellevabienconotraspersonas — *He gets on well with others.*

d. Yomesientosola — *I feel lonely.*

e. Ellosloacosan — *They bully him.*

f. Elloscantanparapasareltiempo — *They sing to pass the time.*

g. Yocreoqueelmatrimonioesimportante — *I think marriage is important.*

h. Mantenerunarelaciónfeliz — *To maintain a happy relationship.*

9. Split sentences.

Yo paso	casada.
Mi amigo	son pobres.
Mi padre me	tiempo allí.
Ella no está	divorciados.
Ellos son	amigos.
Muchos	me escucha.
Ella vive	entiende.
Ellos están	sola.

10. Put the words below in the correct order.

a. son Ellos no pobres: ___________

b. vive Él con madre su: ___________

c. a Ellos menudo molestan lo: ___________

d. nuevos hace amigos Ella: ___________

e. veces A él se solo siente: ___________

f. menudo a discuten Ellos: ___________

11. Translate into English.

a. Discuto a menudo con mi hermana.

b. Vivo con mi padrastro.

c. Ellos me molestan mucho.

d. Me llevo bien con ellos.

e. No me entienden.

f. Me siento solo.

12. Translate into English.

a. Él tiene cuatro hijos, dos niños y dos niñas.

b. Ella es muy trabajadora y ambiciosa.

c. Son una familia pobre pero feliz.

d. Vivo con mis padres y mi hermana.

e. Ella no se lleva bien con ellos.

f. Él ha sido acosado por otros alumnos.

g. Por suerte, ya no se siente solo y triste.

h. Hace dos años él trabajaba en un restaurante.

i. Ellos enviaron a su hijo a un orfanato.

j. Ellas se divirtieron cantando y bailando.

k. No quiero hablar de esto con mis padres.

l. Tengo que intentar estar tranquilo todo el tiempo.

m. Sus padres la apoyan mucho.

n. Quiero casarme en el futuro.

Unit 1 - Higher reading

1. Read this article about Valeria, a girl who lives in an orphanage in Managua, Nicaragua.

> La madre de Valeria es tan pobre que ha enviado a su hija a un orfanato con otros niños. El cambio ha sido duro, pero Valeria está haciendo nuevos amigos, y se divierte con las otras niñas. Duerme en una habitación con otras trece chicas. Las camas son pequeñas pero cómodas y están siempre limpias.
>
> Va a una escuela religiosa. También, a menudo, trabaja en el restaurante del orfanato con las otras alumnas. El dinero que gana en el restaurante se destina al orfanato.
>
> Valeria se lleva bien con los otros niños. Para pasar el tiempo, juegan y cantan juntos.

What does the article say? Put a tick next to each one of three statements made in the article.

a. Valeria's mother is poor.

b. Valeria has to sleep on the ground.

c. Valeria does not go to school.

d. Valeria enjoys making new friends.

e. Valeria often works at a restaurant.

f. Valeria enjoys dancing with the other children.

2. Read this diary extract written by Juan, a boy from Bilbao, in the Basque Country, Spain.

> Hoy ha sido un día bastante bueno en el colegio. Hace algún tiempo, me acosaban mucho. Los otros alumnos se reían de mí por mis gafas y mi forma de hablar. Me sentía triste y solo.
>
> Solía preguntarme por qué los demás reaccionaban así. ¿Era porque yo era diferente? ¿Porque no era tan fuerte o popular como ellos? Tal vez pensaran que era divertido hacerme daño.
>
> No quería decírselo a mis padres porque ya tenían bastante de qué preocuparse. Era difícil levantarme cada mañana e ir al cole sabiendo que tendría que pasar otro día con alumnos que no me aceptaban.
>
> Sin embargo, las cosas han cambiado. Poco a poco, he empezado a hacer amigos que me entienden y me aceptan. Ahora, no me siento tan solo y me doy cuenta de que hay gente que me valora por quien soy.
>
> Siento esperanza por el futuro. Sé que no será fácil, pero tengo la confianza de que las cosas seguirán mejorando. Estoy decidido a mantenerme fuerte y positivo y a disfrutar de los buenos momentos que están por venir.

a. What happened at school today? _______________________________________

b. How did Juan feel in the past? Mention two points.

(i) _______________________________________

(ii) _______________________________________

c. What did Juan not understand? _______________________________________

d. Why did he not speak to his parents? _______________________________________

e. How does Juan feel now? _______________________________________

f. What will he be like in the future? Mention two points. (i) _______________________________________

(ii) _______________________________________

Unit 1 - Higher reading

3. Read this message about what Juan Carlos wrote for a school project.

Nuestro profesor de español nos pidió que escribiéramos un artículo sobre alguien a quien respetáramos de verdad. Así que decidí escribir algo sobre mi tío Ricardo. Para mí, es un modelo a seguir.

Hoy, Ricardo trabaja para una asociación que lucha contra la pobreza. Cuando era adolescente, él no sabía qué hacer y, de hecho, no trabajaba mucho. Después de estudiar en la universidad, quiso encontrar un trabajo interesante que le permitiera ayudar a los demás. Admiro lo que hace ahora. Sé que cada uno tiene que encontrar su propia identidad, pero a mí también me gustaría hacer un trabajo así.

Put a tick next to each one of the two correct statements.

a. Ricardo works for a medical charity.

b. Ricardo worked hard at school.

c. Ricardo attended university.

d. Juan Carlos would like to do the same as Ricardo.

4. Read these five opinions about marriage.

Benjamín

Creo que el matrimonio representa el amor y la fe: nunca hay que mentirse el uno al otro. Vivir con la persona a la que amas es un sueño para mí.

Martina

El matrimonio no es necesario. Se puede amar a alguien y vivir juntos sin casarse. Me gustaría vivir en pareja sin poner mi nombre en un documento oficial.

Felipe

El matrimonio puede ser difícil. A veces la gente siente que ya no es independiente. Las parejas tienen que esforzarse mucho para que su relación siga siendo feliz.

Sofía

Quiero casarme algún día, pero sé que en un matrimonio no todo es perfecto. Hay que aprender a convivir y a escuchar al otro.

Agustín

Cuando mis padres se separaron, fue difícil. Me dije a mí mismo que nunca me casaría. Desde entonces, he cambiado de opinión y estoy abierto a la idea de casarme.

Who said...?

a. Some people feel that their freedom is limited by marriage.   _____________

b. You should never lie to your partner.   _____________

c. They have altered their opinion about marriage.   _____________

d. You can live together without being married.   _____________

e. You have to listen to your partner.   _____________

Unit 1 - Higher reading

5. Read Julieta's description of her best friend.

> Mi mejor amiga se llama María. La conozco desde hace tres años. Es una persona extraordinaria, muy sensible y responsable. Siempre está alegre y llena de energía y me hace sentir especial.
>
> Creo que nuestra amistad viene de nuestros intereses comunes. A las dos nos encanta la música y pasamos horas escuchando juntas nuestras canciones favoritas. A María también le apasiona leer, como a mí, y a menudo compartimos libros y comentamos lo que hemos leído. A veces es muy graciosa y nos reímos mucho juntas. Además, siempre está ahí para mí, dispuesta a escucharme y apoyarme en los momentos difíciles. María es mucho más que una amiga, es como una hermana para mí.

    a. How is María's personality described? Mention three points.

____

    b. What is Julieta's friendship with María based on?

____

    c. Mention two pastimes they have in common.

____

    d. In the second paragraph, what else does Julieta like about María? Mention two details.

____

6. Read Ricardo's description of an ideal friend. Then tick the four correct statements.

> Un amigo ideal es alguien que es amable y siempre está ahí para ti. Te escucha cuando hablas y te entiende incluso sin palabras. Te hace reír cuando estás triste y te apoya si tienes problemas personales. También comparte tus intereses y disfruta haciendo cosas contigo.
>
> En mi opinión, un buen amigo también debe ser alguien divertido a quien le gusten las bromas y que siempre cumpla sus promesas. Me gustan las personas independientes pero a las que no les gustan los conflictos, que creen en la igualdad y que no critican demasiado a los demás.

Ricardo's ideal friend...

a.	... would be sporty.	e.	... would talk a lot.
b.	... would be a good listener.	f.	... would be kind.
c.	... would believe in equality.	g.	... would enjoy an argument.
d.	... would like joking.	h.	... would be patient.

Unit 1 - Grammar focus: adjectives

Adjectives are words used to describe or modify the meaning of a noun or pronoun. They tell you more about a person or thing, for example what it's like, how big it is, what colour it is and so on.

Agreement

We say that adjectives **agree** in Spanish. This means that the end of the adjective is often spelled differently, depending on the **gender and number** of the noun or pronoun it refers to.

Look at these examples:

- Mi **padre** es simpátic**o** (my father is nice).   Mi **madre** es simpátic**a** (my mother is nice).
- Mi **amigo** es delgad**o** (my -male- friend is thin).   Mi **amiga** es delgad**a** (my -female- friend is thin).
- Mis **tíos** son gracios**os** (my uncles are funny).   Mis **tías** son gracios**as** (my aunts are funny).
- **Ellos** están aburrid**os** (they -male- are bored).   **Ellas** están aburrid**as** (they -female- are bored).

Adjectives ending in -o   (e.g. bonito)
Most Spanish adjectives end in **-o** in the **masculine singular form**. For these adjectives, the rule is as follows:

- **-o** if the noun or pronoun is **masculine singular.**
- **-a** if the noun or pronoun is **feminine singular.**
- **-os** if it is **masculine plural.**
- **-as** if it is **feminine plural.**

Adjectives ending in -e   (e.g. fuerte)
Adjectives ending in **-e** don't change for masculine and feminine singular, and add **-s** for their plural form:

Él es interesant**e**.   **Ella** es interesant**e**.
Ellos son interesant**es**.   **Ellas** son interesant**es**.

Adjectives ending in -r   (e.g. hablador)
Adjectives ending in **-r** gain an **'a'** in feminine singular. You also add **-es** (masc) **/** **-as** (fem) for their plural form:

Él es hablador.   **Ella** es hablador**a**.
Ellos son hablador**es**.   **Ellas** son hablador**as**.

Adjectives ending in consonant   (e.g. azul)
Adjectives ending in **-consonant** don't change either for masculine and feminine singular, and add **-s** for their plural form:

Él es jove**n**.   **Ella** es jove**n**.
Ellos son jóven**es**.   **Ellas** son jóven**es**.

When you write and speak, always think carefully about the ending of an adjective. Does it agree correctly with its noun or pronoun?

Position

In English, adjectives go before a noun, for example 'a nice person' or 'a kind man'. In Spanish, they usually go **after the noun**, for example 'una persona simpática' or 'un hombre amable'.

A small number of common Spanish adjectives often go **before the noun** and change their form based on whether they are in front or after the noun:

Before the noun	After the noun	Translation
Buen (un buen coche)	**Bueno** (un coche bueno)	Good (a good car)
Mal (un mal coche)	**Malo** (un coche malo)	Bad (a bad car)
Primer (el primer hijo)	**Primero** (el hijo primero)	First (the first son)
Tercer (el tercer hijo)	**Tercero** (el hijo tercero)	Third (the third son)
***Gran** (el gran problema)	**Grande** (el problema grande)	Big (the big/great problem)

Gran and grande have different meanings – read below for more info!

Gran VS Grande

When the adjective **grande** is used after the noun, it translates as "big".
e.g. **Una casa grande**   *A big house*

However, if placing "**grande**" before the noun, we need to use the shortened (apocopated) form "**gran**". This short form is used **before** the noun for emphasis, and it translates as "great" or "impressive."
e.g. **Una gran persona**   *A great person*

Comparatives

Look how we use adjectives to compare two things:

- Mi amigo es **más** trabajador **que** yo.   *My friend is **more** hard-working **than** me.*
- Mi hermana es **menos** amable **que** yo.   *My sister is **less** kind **than** me.*
- Los amigos son **tan** importantes **como** la familia.   *Friends are **as** important **as** family.*

Some key irregular comparative adjectives:

- **Mejor(es)**   *Better*   - **Peor(es)**   *Worse*
- **Mayor(es)**   *Older, bigger*   - **Menor(es)**   **Younger, smaller*

'Younger'* can also be translated as 'más joven**'.

Superlatives

This is when one thing stands out from the rest, for example the best, the biggest, the longest. See how this works:

- Él/ella es la persona **más** importante.   *He/she is the **most** important person.*
- Él/ella es la persona **menos** importante.   *He/she is the **least** important person.*

But note the following irregular forms:

- **El/la/los/las… mejor(es)**   *The best*   **El/la/los/las… peor(es)**   *The worst*

e.g. Messi es **el mejor** jugador.   *Messi is **the best** football player.*

- **El peor** día de la semana es el lunes.   ***The worst** day of the week is Monday.*

1. Complete the table (some will stay the same).

Masculine	Feminine
Inteligente	
Trabajador	
Amable	
Gracioso	
Valiente	
Moreno	
Feliz	

2. Circle the correct adjective.

a. Mi padre es *divertido/divertida*.

b. Mi madre es muy *bajo/baja*.

c. Mariana está hoy muy *aburrido/aburrida*.

d. Mis padres son bastante *estrictos/estrictas*.

e. Mi prima es muy *trabajador/trabajadora*.

f. Mis tíos son bastante *valiente/valientes*.

g. Sandra es *mentiroso/mentirosa*.

h. Mis tías son *simpáticos/simpáticas*.

i. Gianfranco es muy *musculoso/musculosa*.

3. Complete the translation.

a. Mi madre es ____________   *My mother is strict.*

b. Mi hermana es __________   *My sister is talkative.*

c. Mi madre está __________   *My mother is happy.*

d. Ella parece ______________   *She looks sad.*

e. Mis tíos son ____________   *My uncles are annoying.*

f. Tu madre es ____________   *Your mother is kind.*

g. Ellos son ________________   *They are hard-working.*

4. Complete the translation

a. Un ________ amigo   *A good friend*

b. Un _______ problema   *A small problem*

c. En __________ lugar   *In first place*

d. Un ________ amigo   *A bad friend*

e. Un ________ amigo   *A great friend*

f. Una persona _______   *A sad person*

g. Una persona _______   *A happy person*

h. Una persona _______   *A brave person*

5. Arrange the words in each sentence in the correct order.

a. es Mi estricto padre que mi madre menos   *My father is less strict than my mother.*

b. yo hermana más Mi fuerte es que   *My sister is stronger than me.*

c. son Mis padres más que tíos amables mis   *My parents are kinder than my uncles.*

d. tan nosotros Nuestros altos primos son como   *Our cousins are as tall as us.*

e. trabajador soy mi Yo que más hermano   *I am more hard-working than my brother.*

f. Mi tan es mayor como abuelo abuela mi   *My grandfather is as old as my grandmother.*

6. Tangled translation: translate the English into Spanish.

a. Ella es *smaller* que yo.

b. Yo soy *less intelligent than* mi hermano.

c. Él es más *hard-working* que mi *brother*.

d. Mis tíos son *nicer* que mis tías.

e. Mi hermano es *more* alto *than* mi hermana.

f. Mi padre es *less strict* que mi *mother*.

g. Mi madre es *as* estricta *as* mi padre.

7. Correct the mistake found in the part of the sentence underlined.

a. Mi madre es tan <u>mejor</u> como mi tía.

b. Es un problema <u>gran</u>.

c. Mi primo es tan <u>más inteligente</u> como mi prima.

d. Mis padres son más <u>simpático</u> que mis tíos.

e. Ella es <u>más menor</u> que yo.

f. Nosotros somos más <u>trabajadoras</u> que vosotros.

g. Mis hermanos son <u>más buenos</u> que sus hermanos.

8. Translate into English.

a. Un hombre fuerte: _______________

b. Una mujer alta: _______________

c. Una mujer mayor: _______________

d. Un coche grande: _______________

e. Un chico guapo: _______________

f. Un nuevo amigo: _______________

g. Una casa bonita: _______________

h. Un gran problema: _______________

i. Un hombre mayor: _______________

j. Un profesor nuevo: _______________

k. Un buen amigo: _______________

9. Tick the grammatically correct phrases and, if they are wrong, correct them.

English	Spanish	√/x
A beautiful face	*Un cara bonita*	
A tall man	*Un hombre alto*	
A good-looking boy	*Un chica guapo*	
A small child	*Una niño pequeño*	
A long street	*Una calle larga*	
A new house	*Un casa nuevo*	
A nice person	*Una persona simpática*	
A tall woman	*Una mujer alta*	
A big car	*Un coche grande*	

10. Translate into Spanish (f = feminine and m = masculine).

a. Sister _________ i. Good (f) _________

b. Father _________ j. Tall (m) _________

c. Uncle _________ k. Beautiful (f) _________

d. Brother _________ l. good (m) _________

e. Grandfather _________ m. Big (f) _________

f. Grandmother _________ n. New (f) _________

g. Cousin (f) _________ o. Young (f) _________

h. Aunt _________ p. Small (f) _________

11. Translate into Spanish.

a. A tall man: _______________

b. A small boy: _______________

c. A beautiful face: _______________

d. An old woman: _______________

e. A big car: _______________

f. An old man: _______________

g. A good-looking girl: _______________

h. A new friend (m): _______________

12. Translate into Spanish.

a. My mother is tall, but my sister is taller than her.

____

b. My father is strict, and my mother is as strict as him.

____

c. My grandfather is 73 years old. My grandmother is younger than him.

____

d. My name is Pablo. I am short, but my girlfriend is shorter than me.

____

e. My brother is bigger and taller than me, but I am stronger.

____

f. I have some good teachers (m), but my Spanish teacher (m) is the best. Of course.

____

Unit 1 - Preparing for speaking and writing

1. Complete with the missing letters.

a. A_i_o   *Friend*

b. G_ac_oso   *Funny*

c. Ma_ r _moni_   *Marriage*

d. _po_ar   *To support*

e. A_ab_e   *Kind*

f. A_to   *Tall*

g. B_e_o   *Good*

h. Tra_aj_dor   *Hard-working*

2. Gapped translation.

a. *My father is kind*   Mi padre es ____________.

b. *I get on with him*   Yo me ___________ bien con él.

c. *He is stricter than me*   Él es ________ estricto que yo.

d. *But he is hard-working*   Pero él es ___________.

e. *He is also funny*   Él también es __________.

f. *He tells a lot of jokes*   Él cuenta muchas ___________.

g. *My mother is young*   Mi madre es ____________.

h. *She has a beautiful face*   Ella tiene una cara ___________.

i. *She is not very talkative*   Ella no es muy _____________.

3. Broken words.

a. Short (m): b _ _ _

b. Fun: diver_ _ _ _

c. I live: yo vi_ _

d. I get on: yo me ll_ _ _

e. He is funny: él _ _ gr_ _ _ _ _ _

f. In my family: en mi fam_ _ _ _

g. A good father: un b_ _ _ padre

h. A good mother: una bu_ _ _ madre

i. Hard-working (m): trab_ _ _ _ _ _

4. Tangled translation: translate the English into Spanish.

a. Un *friend* ideal cumple sus *promises*.

b. Un amigo ideal te *supports* todo el *time*.

c. En *my* familia *there are* cuatro *persons*.

d. Mi *best* amigo *is called* Jaime. Él es muy *funny*.

e. *When* yo salgo *with* mis amigos, *we go* a la discoteca.

f. Mi madre es *more strict than* mi padre.

g. *Yesterday* yo *went* a un restaurante con *my parents*.

h. *Two days ago* nosotros fuimos *to the cinema*.

i. Yo *rarely argue* con mis padres.

5. Anagrams.

a. Maidro (husband): ___________

b. mAiog (friend): ___________

c. virtiDoed (fun): ___________

d. aFimlia (family): ___________

e. aAmleb (kind): ___________

f. Viivr (to live): ___________

g. asPra (to spend): ___________

h. oyaApr (support): ___________

i. uMeotr (dead): ___________

j. iVeoj (old): ___________

k. roPe (worse): ___________

l. jeMro (better): ___________

6. Guided translation.

a. He is a good friend: É_ e_ u_ b_ _ _ a_ _ _ _.

b. My mother is short: M_ m_ _ _ _ e_ b_ _ _.

c. My father is lazy: M_ p_ _ _ _ e_ v_ _ _

d. I get on with him: Y_ m_ l_ _ _ _ b_ _ _ c_ _ é _.

e. I look like my mother: Y_ m_ p_ _ _ _ _ _ a m_ m_ _ _ _.

f. My brother is taller: M_ h_ _ _ _ _ _ e_ m_ _ a_ _ _.

g. My sister is kind: M_ h_ _ _ _ _ _ e_ a_ _ _ _ _.

h. I like her a lot: E _ _ _ m_ g_ _ _ _ m_ _ _ _.

i. He is older than me: É_ e_ m_ _ _ _ q_ _ y_.

j. We went to the shops: F_ _ _ _ _ a l_ _ t_ _ _ _ _ _.

k. I argue with him: Y_ d_ _ _ _ _ _ c _ _ é _.

l. My girlfriend is tall: M _ n_ _ _ _ e _ a_ _ _.

7. Complete the missing words.

a. En _ _ familia hay cuatro personas.

b. Yo soy mayor _ _ _ mi padre.

c. Mi madre _ _ _ _ _ _ _ Sandra.

d. Mi hermano es más j _ _ _ _ que yo.

e. Un amigo ideal es alguien que _ _ amable.

f. Yo quiero hablar c_ _ mi tío Julían.

g. Lo m _ _ importante es el amor.

h. Mis padres casi _ _ _ _ _ _ _ discuten.

i. Lo _ _ _ más me gusta de mi padre es que es muy trabajador.

8. Split sentences.

En mi familia hay	discuten a menudo.
Un amigo ideal es	fuimos a la piscina.
Mis padres	mi tío.
Mi hermano es más	cinco personas.
Ayer nosotros	admiro es mi padre.
Quiero hablar de	como yo.
Una persona a quien yo	alguien amable.
Mi madre es	llama Fátima.
Él es tan alto	inteligente que yo.
Mi hermana se	muy trabajadora.

9. Correct the Spanish translations. Some sentences are correct.

a. *There are four people* — Hay cinco personas.

b. *They are eating* — Ellos están comiendo.

c. *They are happy* — Ellos están tristes.

d. *They eat vegetables* — Ellos comen carne.

e. *There are two women* — Hay dos hombres.

f. *They are vegan* — Son veganos.

g. *There are three boys* — Hay tres hijos.

h. *They're playing football* — Ellos juegan al golf.

i. *They are sad* — Están enfadados.

10. Correct the spelling and grammar errors.

a. La mejora cosa.

b. Un amigo ideial.

c. Nosotros somos vegano.

d. Ella es una buen madre.

e. Hay cuatro persona.

f. Mi famila y yo.

g. Mis padres se discuten a menudo.

h. Mi madre es travajadora.

i. Lo quien me gusta de él es que es amable.

11. Translate into Spanish.

a. I get on with my parents. They are kind. ______________________

b. I argue sometimes with my parents. ______________________

c. I think that my mother is kind and patient. ______________________

d. The best thing about him is that he supports me. ______________________

e. I spend a lot of time with my family. ______________________

f. We went to the shopping mall. It was fun. ______________________

g. My sister is very nice but very talkative. ______________________

h. He is funnier than my sister, but less hard-working. ______________________

i. I went to the swimming pool with my father. ______________________

Writing and speaking from a photo card

Write something about both of these photos. Write about who you see, where they are and what they are doing. Read out your description.

_________________________________   _________________________________

_________________________________   _________________________________

_________________________________   _________________________________

Answer the following questions related to this topic. Read out your answers.

1. ¿Cómo es tu mejor amigo? Descríbelo.

2. ¿Qué haces con tus amigos?

3. En tu opinión, ¿cómo es un amigo ideal?

4. ¿Qué opinas sobre el matrimonio?

5. ¿Qué has hecho recientemente con tu familia o con tus amigos?

Speaking in a role-play

Look at the instructions on the left as they would appear in a speaking test. Read aloud with a partner the dialogue on the right. Then do the dialogue a second time, changing the answers or questions in bold. Take turns playing the two roles.

Foundation

<table>
<tr><td>

1. Mention one thing about your best friend.

2. What is your friend's personality like? Mention one thing.

3. Ask your friend a question about their family.

4. Describe your mother or father (give one detail).

5. Say what you did last weekend with friends (give one detail).

</td><td>

1. Indica una cosa sobre tu mejor amigo.
   Se llama Juan.

2. ¿Cómo es la personalidad de tu mejor amigo?
   Él es muy amable.

3. ¿Tienes alguna pregunta para mí?
   ¿Tienes hermanos?

4. Háblame de tu padre o madre.
   Mi padre es gracioso.

5. ¿Qué hiciste el fin de semana pasado con tus amigos?
   Jugué al rugby.

</td></tr>
</table>

....

Higher

<table>
<tr><td>

1. Describe your family (give two details).

2. Say what you think is important in a friend (give one opinion and one reason).

3. Ask your friend a question about family.

4. Give one advantage and one disadvantage of living together.

5. Say what you did with your family recently (give one detail).

</td><td>

1. Háblame de tu familia.
   Tengo un hermano mayor que yo.

2. ¿Cómo crees que es un buen amigo?
   Creo que un buen amigo debe ser divertido porque me gustan las bromas.

3. ¿Tienes alguna pregunta para mí?
   ¿Tienes hermanos?

4. ¿Cuáles son en tu opinión las ventajas y las desventajas de vivir en pareja?
   Puedes hacer muchas cosas juntos, pero eres menos independiente.

5. ¿Qué has hecho últimamente con tu familia?
   He ido al cine.

</td></tr>
</table>

Foundation writing

Write about 50 words in Spanish. Write something about each point.

• A good friend.   • What they look like.   • Their character.   • Why you like them.   • What you do together.

1. ____
2. ____
3. ____
4. ____
5. ____

Using your knowledge of grammar complete the sentences below, choosing one of the three options given.

1. Yo _____________ al centro de la ciudad con mis amigos (vamos/vas/voy).

2. Nosotros _____________ a videojuegos juntos (jugamos/jugar/juego).

3. Yo creo que mi madre es muy _____________ (gracioso/graciosa/graciosos).

4. Mi cantante favorito ha sacado una canción _____________ (nuevo/nueva/nueve).

5. Mis amigos _____________ a menudo de fiesta (salgo/sale/salen).

Foundation/Higher writing

Write approximately 90 words in Spanish. You must refer to each bullet point.

• Your family.   • What you have done recently as a family.   • What you will do in the future as a family.

____
____
____
____
____
____
____

Higher writing

In your exercise book or on paper, write approximately 150 words about relationships. You must write something about all the bullet points. You can either refer to the language in this unit, for example the sentence bank, or do the task in exam conditions, without help. Or you could do both!

- The importance of having friends.
- What you have done recently with your friends.
- The pros and cons of getting married.
- Your future relationship plans.

Foundation sentence bank

Hay cinco personas en mi familia.	There are five people in my family.
Tengo una hermana y un hermanastro.	I have a sister and a stepbrother.
Yo me llevo bien con mis padres.	I get on with my parents.
En mi opinión los amigos son tan importantes como la familia.	In my opinion friends are as important as family.
Mi mejor amigo se llama Sergio.	My best friend is called Sergio.
Tengo un montón de amigos/as en la escuela.	I have lots of friends at school.
Mi amiga Natalia es tranquila y tímida.	My friend Natalia is quiet and shy.
Ella escucha a los demás y acepta a todos.	She listens to others and accepts everyone.
Yo nací en Quito, Ecuador.	I was born in Quito, Ecuador.
El fin de semana pasado jugué al fútbol con mis amigos.	Last weekend I played football with my friends.
A veces discuto con mis hermanos.	Sometimes I argue with my brothers.
Me gusta todo tipo de gente.	I like all sorts of people.
Es importante aceptar ideas diferentes.	It is important to accept different ideas.
Mi madre es graciosa y lista.	My mother is funny and smart.

Higher sentence bank

Yo me llevo bien con mi familia, especialmente con mi madre.	I get on with my family, especially my mother.
Mi madre es graciosa, lista y sensible.	My mother is funny, smart and sensitive.
Discuto con mi hermano de vez en cuando.	I argue with my brother from time to time.
Conozco a mi mejor amigo desde hace tres años.	I have known my best friend for three years.
Mi mejor amigo tiene los mismos intereses que yo.	My best friend has the same interests as me.
Los buenos amigos deben ser amables y pacientes.	Good friends must be kind and patient.
Lo que me gusta es un/a amigo/a que me entienda.	What I like is a friend who understands me.
La conocí jugando al rugby.	I met her while playing rugby.
Mis amigos me hacen reír todo el tiempo.	My friends make me laugh all the time.
Es importante no casarse demasiado joven.	It is important not to get married too young.
Para mí, el matrimonio no es necesario para una pareja.	For me, marriage is not necessary for a couple.
Quiero mantener mi independencia en el futuro.	I wish to keep my independence in the future.
Es importante respetar las diferentes identidades.	It is important to respect different identities.
Me paso horas riendo con mi amigo/a.	I spend hours laughing with my friend.

UNIT 2

The world around us

Contents

- **Foundation vocab building**
- **Foundation reading**
- **Higher vocab building**
- **Higher reading**
- **Grammar focus: using two verbs together**
- **Preparing for speaking and writing**
- **Writing and speaking from a photo card**
- **Speaking in a role play**
- **Writing**
- **Sentence banks**

Unit 2 - Foundation vocab building

Vocabulary

al lado de	next to
el árbol	tree
el barrio	neighbourhood
bonito/a	beautiful
la calle	street
calor	hot
cerca de	close to
el campo	countryside
contaminar	to pollute
la costa	coast
delante de	in front of
derecha	right
detrás	behind
directo	straight
el dormitorio	bedroom
el edificio	building
entre	between
el espacio	space
la fábrica	factory
fabricar	to manufacture
frío	cold
la granja	farm
la habitación	room
el invierno	winter
la isla	island
izquierda	left
el jardín	garden
joven	young
lejos de	far from
limpio/a	clean
la lluvia	rain
el lugar	place
el mar	sea
mejorar	to improve
la montaña	mountain
la niebla	fog
la orilla (del mar)	seashore
la panadería	bakery
el paro	unemployment
pasear	to go for a walk
la playa	beach
la pobreza	poverty
la primavera	spring
el pueblo	town
el salón	living room
seguro/a	safe
situado	situated
el sol	sun
sucio/a	dirty
el tiempo	weather
el verano	summer
el viento	wind

1. Match up.

Limpio	Hot
Sucio	Right
Lejos	Left
Bonito	Young
Joven	Cold
Viejo	Beautiful
Izquierda	Old
Derecha	Poor
Calor	Dirty
Frío	Far
Pobre	Clean

2. Correct the wrong translations.

a. En el campo.	In the city.
b. Hay niebla.	It's windy.
c. En la costa.	On the seaside.
d. Junto al mar.	By the river.
e. Hay un bosque.	There is a factory.
f. Siete dormitorios.	Seven rooms.
g. Hay árboles.	There are flowers.
h. Delante de la casa.	In the house.
i. Hace frío.	It is hot.

3. One of three: circle the right answer.

Verano	Summer	Winter	Spring
Lejos	Near	Far	Behind
Invierno	Autumn	Summer	Winter
Izquierda	Right	Straight	Left
Mar	River	Sea	Beach
Playa	Beach	Play	Sea
Bonito	Windy	Quiet	Beautiful
Derecha	Right	Left	Under
Calle	Shop	Island	Street
Sucio	Sale	Dirty	Salt

4. Tick the words to do with weather.

a. Calor

b. Paro

c. Viento

d. Niebla

e. Frío

f. Salón

g. Lluvia

h. Mar

i. Izquierda

5. Complete the translation.

a. Está detrás de mi casa: *It is __________ my house.*

b. Entre los dos edificios: *____________ the two buildings.*

c. Siempre hace buen tiempo: *The weather is always __________.*

d. Hay muchos espacios verdes: *There are many green __________.*

e. El pueblo es limpio y tranquilo: *The town is ________ and quiet.*

f. Vivo junto al mar: *I live by the __________.*

6. Translate into English.

a. Sol ________

b. Barrio ________

c. Tiempo ________

d. Habitación ________

e. Joven ________

f. Fábrica ________

g. Vivir ________

h. Playa ________

i. Lluvia ________

j. Invierno ________

k. Mar ________

l. Campo ________

7. Sentence puzzle: put the words in the right order.

a. mucho paro Hay

There is a lot of unemployment.

____

b. invierno frío y hace En muy llueve menudo a

In winter it is cold and it rains very often.

____

c. hay cubos No de suficientes en basura las calles

There aren't enough rubbish bins on the streets.

____

d. La en más campo tranquila el y es vida saludable

Life in the countryside is calmer and healthier.

____

e. hay En ruido pueblo mucho mi

In my town there is a lot of noise.

____

f. Mi y está es lugares región históricos bonita llena de

My region is beautiful and full of historic places.

____

g. Mi barrio tranquilo es seguro bastante y

My neighbourhood is quite quiet and safe.

____

8. Complete with the correct option.

a. Hace ____________ en invierno.

b. Mi ciudad es muy ____________.

c. Vivo en el __________ de España.

d. Mi __________ se llama Pavones.

e. Yo vivo en el _____________.

f. Hay varios ___________ históricos.

g. Hay un _____________ pequeño.

h. Yo _____________ la ciudad al campo.

grande
sur
supermercado
barrio
frío
prefiero
lugares
campo

9. Translate into Spanish.

a. I would like to live.

b. There are too many buildings.

c. My neighbourhood is poor.

d. My city is pretty and clean.

e. We can play sports.

f. I go for a walk.

g. The weather is very nice in the spring.

h. There is less noise.

10. Tick all the words with negative meaning.

a. Bonito

b. Contaminación

c. Aburrido

d. Sucio

e. Limpio

f. Seguro

g. Horrible

h. Violento

i. Lluvia

j. Malo

k. Peligroso

11. Translate into English.

a. Es una gran ciudad interesante para los turistas.

b. Hay un centro comercial pequeño cerca de nuestra casa.

c. La vida en el campo es mucho más tranquila y segura.

d. El transporte público es rápido y barato.

e. Me gusta dar un paseo por el bosque.

f. Hay muchas actividades para los jóvenes.

g. Mi barrio es bastante peligroso.

h. No hay muchos árboles ni espacios verdes.

i. En mi región hace buen tiempo en verano y frío en invierno.

j. Vivo en un edificio bastante antiguo en el centro de la ciudad.

k. Prefiero vivir en la ciudad porque la vida en el campo es demasiado tranquila.

Unit 2 - Foundation reading

1. Read these comments from young people about their city.

Mario
Mi barrio es bastante agradable. Hay un supermercado pequeño cerca y mi instituto no está lejos.

Samuel
El transporte público es rápido y no es demasiado caro, así que puedo ir a trabajar muy fácilmente.

Juana
Creo que hay demasiada contaminación en mi ciudad. Me gustaría vivir en un pueblo tranquilo en el campo.

Who says what? Put a cross in the correct column for each question.

Who says...	Mario	Samuel	Juana
a. There is too much pollution.			
b. Their neighbourhood is pleasant.			
c. Public transport is cheap.			
d. They would like to live in the countryside.			
e. School is not far away.			
f. It is easy to get to work.			

2. Read this online message from Francisco.

Me gusta vivir en un pueblo tranquilo en el campo porque es fácil conocer a otras personas y a mí me gusta la gente del campo. Además, me encanta pasear por el bosque con mis amigos. Hay menos ruido que en la ciudad y la naturaleza siempre está cerca. Mi hermano prefiere la gran ciudad. Dice que hay muchas más actividades culturales.

Complete the gap in each sentence using a word from the box below. There are more words than gaps.

forest	quiet	nice	mountains
noise	beautiful	pollution	happy

a. Francisco's village is _______________.

b. He likes walking in the _______________.

c. He thinks that in the city there is more _______________.

d. He says people in the countryside are _______________.

Unit 2 - Foundation reading

3. Read what these people think about living in Mexico DF, the capital of Mexico.

Sandra
Me encanta vivir aquí. Creo que la gente vive feliz. Sin embargo, hay demasiada contaminación.

Mateo
Lo que más me gusta son todas las actividades culturales que se pueden hacer. Creo que es genial.

Adriana
En mi opinión, las personas locales no son muy amables. También hay algunas zonas bastante peligrosas.

Sebastián
Es una gran ciudad para los turistas. No obstante, hay demasiada violencia en algunas zonas.

If the person has a positive opinion put P in the box. If they have a negative opinion put N in the box. If they express both a positive and negative opinion put P/N in the box.

Sandra [ ]   Mateo [ ]   Adriana [ ]   Sebastián [ ]

4. Read this hotel advertisement.

Pequeño hotel tradicional en el casco antiguo, a 500 metros de la estación de bus.

Dieciocho habitaciones y un pequeño aparcamiento de pago enfrente.

Se sirven desayunos y cenas.

Ideal para parejas sin niños. No se admiten perros.

Tick the three correct statements.

   a. The hotel is in an old district.

   b. It is 500m from the city centre.

   c. You can park opposite the hotel.

   d. Breakfast is available.

   e. Dogs are allowed at the hotel.

   f. The hotel would suit families with children.

Unit 2 - Foundation reading

5. **Read what María Isabel says about her village in Equatorial Guinea, Africa. Then answer the questions in English.**

En mi pueblo hay doscientas personas. A menudo hay fiestas en las que la gente canta y baila mucho.

La playa está a tres kilómetros del pueblo. Los hombres van a pescar *(to fish)*. Los fines de semana, a los niños les gusta bañarse en el mar.

Por último, hay una escuela para niños y niñas.

a. How many people live in her village? _________________________________

b. What do people often do? Mention two points. _________________________________

c. What do children like to do at the weekend? _________________________________

d. What does María Isabel say about the school? _________________________________

6. **You see an advert for three places to visit in Cartagena, a city in Colombia. Answer the questions in English.**

✓ Visita el Museo Histórico de Cartagena. Situado en un palacio del siglo XVIII, visitarlo cuesta 24.000 pesos colombianos para los adultos. El edificio es grande y muy bonito.

✓ También debes ir al barrio de Getsemaní con sus casas tradicionales pintadas en varios colores. También hay muchos restaurantes.

✓ No te olvides del Castillo de San Felipe de Barajas. Está en una zona verde pero da mucho el sol ¡así que puede hacer mucho calor!

a. Where is the museum situated? _________________________________

b. What does the advert say about the building? Mention two details.

(i) _______________________   (ii) _______________________

c. What can you find in the Getsemaní neighbourhood? Mention two details.

(i) _______________________   (ii) _______________________

d. How would you translate "da mucho el sol"? _________________________________

7. **Read this short description of a town. Then circle the best option in each case.**

La ciudad es antigua y muy bonita. Hay un jardín público y a todo el mundo le encanta el museo histórico. No hay estación de tren, pero hay muchos autobuses. Es ideal para ir de compras.

1. The town is...   a. modern   b. old   c. large

2. There is no...   b. train station   b. cathedral   c. town square

3. It's great for...   a. shopping   b. walking   c. sight-seeing

Unit 2 - Higher vocabulary building

Vocabulary

el árbol	*tree*
afuera	*outside*
las afueras	*suburb(s)*
alquilar	*to rent*
alrededor (de)	*around*
anciano/a	*old (person)*
antiguo/a	*old (object, building)*
apagar	*to switch off*
el barrio	*neighbourhood*
la basura	*rubbish*
la calle	*street*
el campo	*countryside*
cerca (de)	*near*
el/la ciudadano/a	*citizen*
conducir	*to drive*
construir	*to build*
la costa	*coast*
cruzar	*to cross*
delante (de)	*in front of*
detrás (de)	*behind*
el edificio	*building*
encender	*to switch on*
entre	*between*
el estado	*state*
la fábrica	*factory*
fabricar	*to manufacture*
la falta (de)	*lack (of)*
la isla	*island*
lejos (de)	*far*
limpio/a	*clean*
llover	*to rain*
el lugar	*place*
mejorar	*to improve*
parar	*stop*
pobre	*poor*
la pobreza	*poverty*
el país	*country*
el paisaje	*landscape*
peor	*worse*
lo peor	*the worst*
la preocupación	*concern*
la riqueza	*wealth*
el río	*river*
seguro/a	*safe*
sucio/a	*dirty*
el tiempo	*time, weather*
vender	*to sell*
venir	*to come*
vivir	*to live*

1. Match up.

Árbol	Countryside
Río	Flower
Isla	Landscape
Campo	Tree
Paisaje	Place
Calle	River
Lugar	Near
Flor	Far
Cerca	Coast
Lejos	Neighbourhood
Barrio	Street
Costa	Island

2. Correct the wrong translations.

a. Conducir: *To throw*

b. Apagar: *To switch off*

c. Encender: *To switch on*

d. Fabricar: *To save*

e. Vender: *To cut*

f. Visitar: *To sell*

g. Construir: *To build*

h. Mejorar: *To like*

i. Vivir: *To move*

3. One of three: circle the right answers.

Afuera	*Outside*	*Inside*	*Behind*
Entre	*Opposite*	*Between*	*Entry*
Falta	*Poor*	*Island*	*Lack*
Pobre	*Rich*	*Silly*	*Poor*
Paisaje	*Landscape*	*Country*	*City*
Peor	*Nicer*	*Worse*	*Better*
País	*Country*	*Money*	*Tree*
Árbol	*Place*	*Tree*	*Flower*
Cerca	*Near*	*Far*	*At*
Costa	*Cute*	*Coast*	*Coat*
Sucio	*Clean*	*Nice*	*Dirty*

4. Spot and translate the verbs on the list below.

a. Peor

b. Detrás

c. Eliminar

d. Alquilar

e. Árbol

f. Limpiar

g. Vivir

h. Barrio

i. Llover

5. Complete the translations.

a. El paisaje es muy bonito: the ____________ is very beautiful.

b. Ellos venden productos locales: they ____________ local products.

c. Nosotros vivimos cerca de la costa: we live near the ____________.

d. Mi barrio está limpio: my neighbourhood is ____________.

e. Llueve todo el tiempo: it ____________ all the time.

f. Es un pueblo bastante tranquilo: it is quite a ____________ town.

g. Un río cruza la ciudad: a river ____________ the city.

h. El centro de la ciudad está lejos: the city centre is ____________.

i. Mi preocupación es la contaminación: my ____________ is pollution.

j. Hay demasiado ruido aquí: there is too much ____________ here.

k. Mi región es bastante pobre: my region is quite ____________.

---

6. Match the opposites.

Peor	Encender
Comprar	Grande
Apagar	Abrir
Frío	Mejor
Pequeño	Limpio
Ir	Nuevo
Sucio	Volver
Antiguo	Vender
Cerrar	Calor

7. Circle the correct option.

a. Vivo en la *edificio/cerca/orilla* del mar.

b. Es un *casa/lugar/fábrica* turístico.

c. El *peor/paisaje/costa* es muy bonito.

d. No está *lugar/limpio/cerca* de Valencia.

e. Mi *ciudad/barrio/tienda* está limpio.

f. Hay muchos espacios *rojas/azul/verdes.*

g. Hay muchos *gente/flores/lugares* históricos.

h. Ellos plantan *árboles/coches/islas.*

i. Lo peor es el *falta/ruido/lejos.*

8. Missing letters.

a. R_ido — *Noise*

b. Árb_l — *Tree*

c. Su_io — *Dirty*

d. _ábrica — *Factory*

e. Lu_ar — *Place*

f. Ca_le — *Street*

g. R_o — *River*

h. Lo p_or — *The worst*

i. Fal_a — *Lack*

---

9. Unjumble the words and translate.

a. iucdda: ciudad city

b. scuio ________ ________

c. llaec: ________ ________

d. pomca: ________ ________

e. eeecdnnr: ________ ________

f. eerdvn: ________ ________

g. mprocra: ________ ________

h. ulgra: ________ ________

10. Break the flow. Insert lines where there should be gaps.

a. Lopeorenmiciudadeselruidoyeltráfico.

b. Vivoenelcampo,bastantelejosdelcentrodelaciudad.

c. Porlanocheenciendentodaslasluces.¡Esprecioso!

d. Pormiciudadpasaunrío.

e. Haymuchosárbolesyzonasverdes.

f. Hayunfestivaldemúsicamuyfamoso.

g. Tambiénhaymuchoslugareshistóricosparavisitar.

h. Lopeoresqueeltransportepúbliconoesnadabueno.

---

11. Complete with the correct verb from the ones in the grid.

a. Yo ____________ en el campo.

b. La tienda ________ productos locales.

c. No ____________ una ciudad rica.

d. Siempre __________ calor.

e. En verano ________ sol todos los días.

f. Nosotros __________ salir en barco.

g. Ellos ____________ muchos edificios.

h. ____________ mejorar el transporte público.

i. Hay muchos lugares para __________.

j. Podemos __________ senderismo en la montaña.

k. Demasiada gente ________ en coche.

l. Yo nunca ____________ al campo.

deben	es	construyen	vivo
hace	hacer	podemos	vende
visitar	va	voy	hace

12. Translate into English.

a. Me gusta vivir aquí porque la gente es amable y simpática.

b. Vivo en Cochabamba desde hace unos años.

c. Debemos mejorar el transporte público.

d. Hay muchos lugares históricos en nuestra región.

e. Hay muchas personas pobres y sin hogar.

f. Después de ir al cine, comimos en un restaurante.

g. Decidí pasar el día en la playa.

h. Antes vivía en Puebla pero ahora vivo en Cancún.

i. Debemos reciclar para proteger el medioambiente.

j. Espero vivir en el campo en el futuro.

k. El campo es más tranquilo y seguro que la ciudad.

l. Lo que me gusta es que hay muchas cosas que hacer para los jóvenes.

m. Me gustaría vivir en el extranjero uno o dos años.

n. Admito que hay demasiada contaminación y ruido.

o. Mi región es bastante pobre, pero la gente es muy amable.

Unit 2 - Higher reading

1. **Read about the small town of Boquete in Panama. Then answer the questions in English.**

Boquete se sitúa al oeste de Panamá, a 60 kilómetros de Costa Rica. Boquete está cerca del volcán Barú, un volcán inactivo que es el punto más alto del país. A los turistas les encanta visitar este lugar por su naturaleza: hay un río, plantaciones de café y dos parques nacionales. Además, en este pueblo hay muchos hoteles y restaurantes en los que se puede probar la gastronomía local.

El tiempo es muy bueno, con temperaturas de entre 12°C y *30°C, por lo que Boquete es uno de los lugares más frescos de Panamá. Me gusta vivir aquí porque es un lugar bastante tranquilo, excepto cuando tiene lugar *(takes place)* la Feria de las Flores y del Café en enero. Entonces, llegan muchos visitantes de otros pueblos y ciudades.

**To tell the temperature (using Celsius) in Spanish you can say "grados centígrados" or "grados Celsius". If you are using Fahrenheit you say "grados Fahrenheit". You can also just say "grados" on it's own, and people will know which one you mean, depending on where you are.*

    a.   Where exactly is Boquete? Mention two details.

    b.   Mention two places tourists can visit in the town and surrounding areas.

    c.   How is the climate described? Mention three points.

    d.   Is the town always quiet? Explain.

2. **Read about an event in Tudela, a small city in Navarra, north of Spain.**

Como cada año, la ciudad invita a todos los vecinos a acercarse al centro para conocer todas las asociaciones locales. Si le gusta el deporte, la música o el baile, habrá algo que le interese.

También puede informarse sobre el trabajo de las asociaciones si quiere ser voluntario, por ejemplo en la biblioteca o con los ancianos, o si quiere ayudar a las personas sin hogar.

Por último, hay actividades gratuitas para niños durante todo el día: juegos, canciones, dibujo, etc.

Circle the best answer to complete each sentence.

1.	This event takes place…	a. twice a year	b. once a year	c. throughout the year
2.	You get to know about…	a. job opportunities	b. concerts	c. clubs and charities
3.	It will interest those who want to…	a. volunteer	b. work	c. visit the town centre
4.	You might want to help…	a. the unemployed	b. the homeless	c. disabled people

Unit 2 - Higher reading

3. Read this message from Farah, a young Moroccan woman.

¡Qué suerte tengo! Me gusta mucho vivir aquí, en El Escorial, al norte de Madrid, porque no estoy lejos del centro de la capital y el transporte público es rápido. Hace cinco años vivía en Huelva, en el suroeste de España, pero vine a El Escorial por un nuevo trabajo.

En cuanto a mi marido, va a empezar un nuevo trabajo en Toledo el mes que viene. Pienso que nos mudaremos allí y compraremos un piso pequeño. De todas formas, no me importa, porque me encanta moverme, cambiar de trabajo y descubrir nuevas regiones

What does the article say about these events? In each box, write P for something that happened in the past, N for something that is happening now, F for something that will happen in the future.

a. Living in Toledo

b. Living in Huelva

c. Living in El Escorial

d. Buying a flat

4. Read what Marco says about environmental issues in a region of Argentina.

En nuestra región del sur de Argentina, los problemas medioambientales son cada vez más graves. La producción de energía es más limpia, pero la contaminación atmosférica causada por vehículos y fábricas sigue afectando la salud de nuestros habitantes.

Además, hay demasiados residuos plásticos en nuestros ríos y bosques, lo que pone en peligro a los animales.

Ante estos retos, es importante actuar ahora. Tenemos que utilizar menos plástico y proteger los bosques. Trabajando juntos, podemos proteger el medioambiente de nuestra región.

In English, write relevant information from the article.

a. Energy production.

____

b. A cause of health problems.

____

c. A threat to animal species.

____

d. What should be done now. Mention two points.

____

Unit 2 - Higher reading

5. Read this article about transport in Vitoria-Gasteiz, in the north of Spain. Answer the questions in English.

La ciudad de Vitoria-Gasteiz es conocida desde hace mucho tiempo por su trabajo en el área de la sostenibilidad, especialmente en el ámbito del transporte público. Tanto residentes como visitantes pueden desplazarse fácilmente gracias a las bicicletas de alquiler y los autobuses de la ciudad, incluidos los servicios exprés. Estos autobuses circulan de día y de noche.

Los vecinos y turistas también pueden compartir su coche y alquilar coches eléctricos. Incluso puede utilizar el tranvía para desplazarse por la ciudad. Para los distritos con menos habitantes, existe el Transporte a Demanda (TAD), que permite a los residentes reservar plazas en un minibús. En 2024, la ciudad introdujo nuevos autobuses eléctricos.

a. What is Vitoria-Gasteiz known for? _________________________________

b. What is said about bus services? _________________________________

c. Why is the tram mentioned? _________________________________

d. What is TAD? _________________________________

e. Where is TAD used? _________________________________

6. Read what Alejo says about his local area. Then circle the best option in each case.

Me gusta aprovechar todas las oportunidades que ofrece mi ciudad. La semana pasada, antes de ir al cine en el centro de la ciudad, mis amigos y yo fuimos a un restaurante peruano nuevo frente a la estación de tren.

Los domingos la ciudad está tranquila. Por eso, hace dos semanas mi novia y yo fuimos a pasear por un jardín público muy bonito que tiene un pequeño lago. Allí se puede ir en barca (rowboat).

También me interesa la vida cultural, así que el lunes decidí ir a un concierto en el teatro de la ciudad. Este teatro se construyó hace 50 años, y casi todas las noches hay un espectáculo para adultos o niños. Hay que reservar con antelación, ya que las entradas suelen agotarse con rapidez.

1. Alejo went to the cinema… a. last week b. last weekend c. on Sunday

2. The restaurant is… a. in the town centre b. in a park c. opposite the station

3. Alejo walked… a. in the town centre b. in the park c. by the river

4. The theatre has shows… a. almost every night b. just on Mondays c. just for adults

5. What advice is given in the last sentence and why?

____

Unit 2 - Grammar focus: using two verbs together

Phrasal verbs: putting two verbs together

Look at the sentences below:

- *Yo **aprendo a / tocar** la guitarra.*   I **learn / to play** the guitar.
- *Yo **acabo de / tocar** la guitarra.*   I **just / played** the guitar.
- *Yo **puedo / tocar** (bien) la guitarra.*   I **can / play** the guitar (well).

In each sentence there are **two verbs**. This union of two (or more) verbs that function as one verb in a sentence is called **phrasal verb**.

In the Spanish examples the second verb is in the **infinitive**. There are also phrasal verbs in which the second verb is a gerund or a participle but we will focus now on those formed with infinitive.

Phrasal verbs with infinitive: *poder, deber, querer*

These are useful verbs that are **always followed by an infinitive**.

Poder (can/to be able to)

- *Yo **puedo** visitar un castillo*   I **can** visit a castle.
- *Yo **podía** visitar un castillo*   I **was able** to visit a castle.
- *Yo **podría** visitar un castillo*   I **would be able to/might/could** visit a castle.

Deber (to have to/must) or in the conditional **ought to/should**

- *Ella **debe** coger el tren*   She **has to/must** take the train.
- *Ella **debía** coger el tren*   She **had to** take the train.
- *Ella **debería** coger el tren*   She **ought to/should** take the train.

Querer (to want)

- *Yo **quiero** vivir en San José*   I **want** to live in San José.
- *Yo **quería** vivir en San José*   I **wanted** to live in San José.
- *Yo **querría** vivir en San José*   I **would want** to live in San José.

Prepositions

Sometimes the two verbs need to be linked with the word **a, que** or **de** (among other options we won't see now). Look at the two examples below.

*Yo empecé **a** reciclar la basura.*   I started to recycle rubbish.
*Yo tuve **que** comprar un billete nuevo.*   I had to buy a new ticket.

Common verbs followed by *a* + infinitive		Common verbs followed by *de* + infinitive		Common verbs followed by *que* + infinitive	
Aprender	*To learn*	Acabar	*To have just done something*	Haber	*To be necessary - hay*
Empezar	*To start*			Tener	*To have*
Ir	*To go*	Estar a punto	*To be about to do something*		
Volver	*To do smth. again*	Dejar	*To stop/quit*		
		Parar	*To stop*		
		Olvidarse	*To forget*		

1. Match up.

Poder	To wish
Querer	To hope
Deber	To be able to (can)
Odiar	To love
Desear	To want
Preferir	To know (how to)
Amar	To have to (must)
Esperar	To hate
Saber	To prefer

2. Insert the correct verb (in the present tense).

a. Yo __________ visitar un castillo. *Can*

b. Yo __________ ir a la ciudad. *Must*

c. Yo __________ conducir coches. *Know how to*

d. Me __________ vivir en Tegucigalpa. *Like*

e. Mi madre __________ visitar Buenos Aires. *Wants*

f. Mi hermano __________ ganar la competición. *Hopes*

g. Yo __________ vivir en el campo. *Prefer*

h. Nos __________ proteger el medioambiente. *Like*

i. Yo __________ vivir en una ciudad grande. *Hate*

3. Complete the translation.

a. Yo quiero ______________ en Perú. *I want to live in Peru.*

b. Me encanta ____________ castillos. *I love to see castles.*

c. Yo espero ____________ a la playa. *I hope to go to the beach.*

d. Ella va a _______________ en bus. *She's going to travel by bus.*

e. Tú puedes _____________ museos. *You can visit museums.*

f. Yo prefiero _____________ el tren. *I prefer to take the train.*

g. Le _______________ ir al cine. *He likes to go to the cinema.*

4. Translate into Spanish.

a. I like to go:

b. I hope to live:

c. I want to travel:

d. I hope to rent:

e. She must be:

f. We can visit:

g. You (singular) like to have:

5. Arrange the words in each sentence in the correct order.

a. debo Yo ir mañana compras mañana de por la — *I must go shopping tomorrow morning.*

b. ir Tú en amigos barco puedes río con por el — *You can go boating on the river with friends.*

c. a voy Hoy a un comer en italiano restaurante — *Today, I'm going to eat in an Italian restaurant.*

d. nos vivir A gustaría nosotros extranjero en el — *We would like to live abroad.*

e. Yo muchos visitar espero monumentos aquí — *I hope to visit lots of monuments here.*

6. Tangled translation: rewrite in the Spanish.

a. Le *likes to go* a la ciudad *with her* amigas.

b. Yo *want* visitar un *castle* en el *countryside*.

c. Él *knows how to* conducir un *car*.

d. Yo *must recycle* más *clothes*.

e. Mi hermano *wants to live* en la *capital*.

f. Nosotros *hate* ver el *town* contaminado.

g. ¿*Do you prefer* vivir *in the city* o *in the countryside*?

7. Circle and correct the mistakes, including accents.

a. Yo quiero a vivir en Chile.

b. Ellos quieren comen en el restaurante aleman.

c. ¿Odias visitando museos?

d. Yo prefiero que tomar el transporte publico.

e. No me gusta dando clases en la ciudad.

f. Nos encanta a visitar la capital.

g. Mis amigos van ir al teatro el sabado que viene.

8. In each sentence insert *a, de, que* or nothing after the first verb.

a. Yo intento __ probar todos los platos.

b. Me ha empezado __ gustar esta ciudad.

c. Me encanta __ visitar museos.

d. Mi madre aprende __ nadar en la piscina.

e. He decidido __ coger el tren.

f. No tengo __ irme de mi región.

g. Ella odia __ viajar en avión.

h. Yo quiero __ comprar una casa en Madrid.

i. Ayudamos __ reciclar la basura.

j. Espero __ vivir en el extranjero en el futuro.

k. Me he olvidado __ comprar un billete.

9. Tick the grammatically correct phrases and, if they are wrong, correct them.

English	Spanish	✓/X
I try to help.	Intento de ayudar.	
I decided to be.	Decidí ser.	
I began to see.	Empecé de ver.	
I forgot to go.	Me olvidé de ir.	
I learned to speak.	Aprendí hablar.	
I managed to buy.	Conseguí a comprar.	
I just arrived.	Acabo de llego.	
I've just bought.	Acabo de comprar.	
I stopped going.	Dejé a ir.	

10. Different tenses: translate into English.

a. Yo debería vivir: ___________________

b. Yo podría comprar: ___________________

c. Me gustaría ir: ___________________

d. Yo podría vivir: ___________________

e. Yo tuve que irme: ___________________

f. Yo dejé de hacer: ___________________

g. Yo intentaré ir: ___________________

h. Yo quería visitar: ___________________

11. Translate into Spanish.

a. I'll try to visit: ___________________

b. I'd like to buy: ___________________

c. He should stay: ___________________

d. You could leave: ___________________

e. We had to live: ___________________

f. I wanted to go: ___________________

g. I began to like: ___________________

h. I decided to go: ___________________

12. Translate into Spanish.

a. I would like to live in Punta Arenas but I must buy a house in Buenos Aires.

____

b. My brother wishes to live in a flat in Madrid, but he would have to travel to work by car.

____

c. When I decided to visit an old castle in the countryside, my friend refused to accompany me.

____

d. I have just begun to appreciate all the activities in this beautiful city.

____

e. When I was young I wanted to live in Madrid, but now I want to live in Barcelona.

____

f. One can live in the capital if one wants to enjoy all the possible activities.

____

Unit 2 - Preparing for speaking and writing

1. Re-arrange the words in each sentence in the correct order.

a. en un Yo vivo al del lado pueblo mar bonito — *I live in a beautiful town by the sea.*

b. Yo en un antiguo barrio vivo fuera ciudad de la — *I live in an old neighbourhood outside the city.*

c. peor transporte es Lo el público — *The worst thing is public transport.*

d. muchas Hay en tiendas el ciudad de centro la — *There are a lot of shops in the city centre.*

e. diez Nosotros aquí vivido años hemos durante — *We have been living here for ten years.*

f. Me mi gusta pero pueblo hay paro mucho — *I like my town but there is a lot of unemployment.*

g. mayor es la Mi preocupación del aire contaminación — *My biggest concern is air pollution.*

h. vivo Yo la vida en campo el porque tranquila es más — *I live in the countryside because life is quieter.*

2. Gapped translation.

a. En el c__________ de basura. *In the rubbish bin.*

b. Yo reciclo la b__________. *I recycle the rubbish.*

c. Está l__________ de Sevilla. *It is far from Seville.*

d. Yo v______________ en el sur. *I live in the south.*

e. Hay p________. *There's unemployment.*

f. Mi m________ preocupación. *My biggest worry.*

g. La vida en el __________. *Life in the countryside.*

h. Hay menos r________. *There is less noise.*

3. Tangled translation: translate the English into Spanish.

a. Yo *live* en Londres desde hace *fifteen* años.

b. Me encanta el *climate* de esta *region*.

c. La *pollution* es un problema *serious*.

d. Mi *neighbourhood* es bastante *dangerous*.

e. Lo *worst thing* es *the crime*.

f. Mi padre *has found* un trabajo *here*.

g. En mi *street* no hay *shops*.

h. En mi *house* hay seis *rooms*.

4. Translate into Spanish.

a. Here: a_ _í

b. Countryside: c_ _p_

c. Noise: ru_ _ _

d. People: _en_ _

e. House: c_ _a

f. Rubbish: b_s_ _ _

g. Building: e_ _f_ _ _ _

h. Street: ca_ _ _

i. Quiet: t_ _ _ _ _ _ _

j. Beautiful: b_ _i_ _

k. Factories: f_ _r_ _ _ _

l. Unemployment: p_r_

5. Complete.

a. Yo vivo e_ una ciudad pequeña e_ Inglaterra.

b. Cerca d_ mi casa h_ _ varias tiendas y una escuela.

c. Hay muchas cosas q_ _ hacer aquí.

d. Me gusta vivir a_ _ _ porque la g_ _ _ _ es amable.

e. H_ _ quinientos habitantes en m_ pueblo.

f. Me gusta ir a_ cine c_ _ mis amigos.

g. Mi barrio e_ muy agradable y limpio.

h. Hay m_ _ _ _ contaminación en m_ región.

i. El fin de semana pasado yo f_ _ _ la playa.

j. El sábado que viene yo v_ _ a visitar u_ castillo.

k. El domingo pasado yo reciclé la b_ _ _ _ _.

l. H_ _ mucho ru _ _ _ en mi ciudad.

6. Add the missing accents.

a. Mi region es bonita.

b. Tu reciclas la basura.

c. El fue al cine.

d. Yo volvi a Paris despues de diez años.

e. Mi padre trabaja en una fabrica.

f. Me gustaria vivir en el campo.

g. Un rio pasa por la ciudad.

h. Yo empece a ir al mercado.

7. Spot and insert the missing words.

a. El año pasado a Madrid.

b. En mi casa dos baños.

c. Mi mayor preocupación la contaminación.

d. El paisaje alrededor de la ciudad muy bonito.

e. Mi ciudad es muy bonita hay bastante pobreza.

f. Yo nunca la basura.

g. Mi ciudad no hay tiendas.

h. Vivo bastante lejos centro de la ciudad.

8. Complete with the missing letters.

a. E_ m_ pu_ _ _o h_ _ mu_ _ _ _ lu_ _ _e_ hi_t_ _ _ _ _s.   *In my town there are lots of historic places.*

b. Y_ v_ _ _ e_ u_ _ gr_ _ c_ _d_ _ in_ _st_ _ _ _.   *I live in a big industrial city.*

c. N_ _ _ _ _ _ _ he_ _ _ viv_ _ _ aq_ _ c_ _ _ _ a_ _ _.   *We have lived here for five years.*

d. L_ c_ _t_ _ _ _ _ _ _ _ e_ u_ p_ _b_ _ _ _ s_ r_ _ a_ _ _.   *Pollution is a serious problem here.*

e. M_ m_ _ _ _ tr_ _ _ _ _ e_ e_ c_ _ _ _o d_ _ p_e_ _ _.   *My mother works in the town centre.*

f. Y_ p_ _ _ _ _ _ _ v_ _ _ _ e_ e_ c_ _ _ _.   *I prefer living in the countryside.*

g. M_ b_ _r_ _ e_ m_ _ agr_ _ _ _ _ _.   *My neighbourhood is very pleasant.*

9. Translate into Spanish.

a. Factories   __________

b. Buildings   __________

c. Rubbish   __________

d. Countryside   __________

e. Beautiful   __________

f. Dangerous   __________

g. Streets   __________

h. Houses   __________

i. Polluted   __________

j. Poverty   __________

k. Unemployment   __________

l. There are   __________

10. Complete with a suitable word.

a. Yo __________ en el campo.

b. En mi __________ hay muchas tiendas.

c. Mi __________ es bastante pobre.

d. Hay muchos __________ históricos.

e. Yo vivo en un __________ pequeño.

f. El paisaje es muy __________ alrededor de mi ciudad.

g. El __________ público no es muy bueno.

h. Hay muchas __________ para hacer.

i. Yo siempre reciclo la __________.

j. Yo vivo en un pueblo bonito en el __________.

11. Translate into Spanish.

a. I have lived in Bilbao for ten years.

b. I live in an old neighbourhood outside the city.

c. On my street there are only two shops.

d. In my town there are few green spaces.

e. There is too much noise and pollution.

f. Too many people drive a car.

g. I would like to live in the countryside.

h. There, life is calmer and there is less crime.

i. The worst thing is that my city is not safe.

j. One day I would like to live abroad, in France.

k. I hope to live in a big city in Italy.

Unit 2 - Writing and speaking from a photo card

Write something about both of these photos in Spanish. Write about who you see, where they are and what they are doing. Read out your description.

____

____

____

Answer the following questions related to this topic. Read out your answers.

1. Describe el pueblo o la ciudad donde vives.

2. ¿Qué haces para proteger el medioambiente?

3. ¿Prefieres la ciudad o el campo? ¿Por qué?

4. ¿Qué has hecho recientemente en tu región?

5. ¿Qué vas a hacer el fin de semana que viene?

Unit 2 - Speaking in a role-play

Look at the instructions on the left as they would appear in a speaking test. With a partner, read aloud the dialogue on the right. Then do the dialogue a second time, changing the answers or questions in bold. Take turns playing the two roles.

Foundation

<table>
<tr><td>

1. Mention one thing about where you live.

2. Say one thing you like to do in your town/village.

3. Ask your friend a question about where they live.

4. Describe your region (give one detail).

5. Say what you do to protect the environment (give one detail).

</td><td>

1. ¿Dónde vives?
   Vivo en Londres.

2. ¿Qué te gusta hacer en tu pueblo o ciudad?
   Me gusta ir al cine.

3. ¿Tienes alguna pregunta para mí?
   ¿Dónde vives?

4. Háblame de tu región.
   Hay bastantes castillos.

5. ¿Qué haces para proteger el medioambiente?
   Reciclo las botellas.

</td></tr>
</table>

Higher

<table>
<tr><td>

1. Say what people can do in your area (give two details).

2. Say if you like living in your area (give one opinion and one reason).

3. Ask your friend a question about where they live.

4. Describe an environmental problem in your area. Give one detail.

5. Say what you did to protect the environment recently (give two details).

</td><td>

1. ¿Qué se puede hacer en tu región?
   Puedes hacer senderismo y visitar castillos.

2. ¿Qué opinas sobre tu región?
   Es una región bonita pero hay un poco de pobreza.

3. ¿Tienes alguna pregunta para mí?
   ¿Te gusta vivir aquí?

4. ¿Hay problemas medioambientales en tu región?
   Sí, los ríos están muy contaminados.

5. ¿Qué has hecho recientemente para cuidar el medioambiente?
   He reciclado ropa y he montado en bicicleta.

</td></tr>
</table>

Unit 2 - Foundation writing

Describe the photo. Write four short sentences in Spanish.

1. ____
2. ____
3. ____
4. ____
5. ____

Foundation/Higher writing

Write to your friend about where you live. You must include the following points:
• Things for young people to do in your area. • Your opinion of the area with a reason. • What you have done recently in your area. • Something you will do in the future in your area. Write about 90 words in Spanish.

____
____
____
____
____
____
____
____
____
____

Higher writing

1. **Write about your city or region for an online magazine. You must include the following points:**
   • Advantages and disadvantages of living where you do. • An environmental issue in your local area or region. • What you have done recently in your area. • What you intend to do in the future.
   Write your answer in Spanish. You should aim to write between 130 and 150 words.

2. **Translate the paragraph below.**
   There are many things to do in my region. However, there is too much pollution in the local rivers. Last week my friends and I went to the cinema in the city centre. Next Sunday I hope to visit a castle in the countryside with my parents. I like to live here because people are kind.

Foundation sentence bank

Vivo en una ciudad pequeña en Inglaterra.	I live in a small city in England.
Cerca de mi casa hay algunas tiendas y una escuela.	Near my home there are some shops and a school.
Hay muchas cosas que hacer aquí.	There are lots of things to do here.
Me gusta vivir aquí porque la gente es simpática.	I like living here because the people are nice.
Hay quinientas personas en mi pueblo.	There are five hundred people in my village.
Me gusta ir al cine con mis amigos.	I like to go to the cinema with my friends.
Mi barrio es muy agradable y limpio.	My neighbourhood is very pleasant and clean.
Hay demasiada contaminación en mi región.	There is too much pollution in my region.
Intento proteger el medioambiente.	I try to protect the environment.
El transporte público es rápido.	Public transport is fast.
El fin de semana pasado fui a la playa.	Last weekend I went to the beach.
En mi opinión, el pueblo es interesante.	In my opinion the town is interesting.
El próximo sábado voy a visitar un castillo.	Next Saturday I am going to visit a castle.
El domingo pasado reciclé alguna ropa.	Last Sunday I recycled some clothes.

Higher sentence bank

Me gustaría vivir aquí porque la gente es simpática.	I would like to live here because people are nice.
Vivo en Chihuahua desde hace dos años.	I have lived in Chihuahua for two years.
Se puede viajar en autobús, metro o tren.	You can travel by bus, metro or train.
Nuestra región es histórica y turística.	Our region is historical and touristy.
Hay mucha gente pobre y sin hogar.	There are many poor and homeless people.
Después de ir al cine, comí en el restaurante.	After going to the cinema, I ate at the restaurant.
Decidí ir a la playa con mis amigos.	I decided to go to the beach with my friends.
Antes vivía en Londres, pero ya no.	Before, I used to live in London but not anymore.
Reciclamos todo para proteger el medioambiente.	We recycle everything to protect the environment.
Espero vivir en el campo en el futuro.	I hope to live in the countryside in the future.
El campo es más tranquilo que la ciudad.	The countryside is quieter than the city.
Me gustaría vivir en el extranjero algún día.	I would like to live abroad one day.
Reconozco que hay demasiada contaminación y ruido.	I recognise that there is too much pollution and noise.
Lo que me gusta son todas las actividades disponibles.	What I like is all of the available activities.

UNIT 3

School and future plans

Contents

- **Foundation vocab building**
- **Foundation reading**
- **Higher vocab building**
- **Higher reading**
- **Grammar focus: contrasting present and past**
- **Preparing for speaking and writing**
- **Writing and speaking from a photo card**
- **Speaking in a role play**
- **Writing**
- **Sentence banks**

Vocabulary	
aburrido/a	*boring*
la actividad	*activity*
aprender	*to learn*
aprobar	*to pass*
la asignatura	*subject*
la carrera	*career, degree*
el colegio/la escuela	*school*
convertirse	*to become*
los deberes	*homework*
difícil	*difficult*
duro/a	*hard*
el edificio	*building*
la elección	*choice*
emocionante	*exciting*
la empresa	*company*
enseñar	*to teach*
el equipo	*team*
esperar	*to hope*
estricto/a	*strict*
estudiar	*to study*
explicar	*to explain*
la fábrica	*factory*
fácil	*easy*
fascinante	*fascinating*
el futuro	*future*
la habilidad	*skill*
igual	*equal*
independiente	*independent*
interesante	*interesting*
inútil	*useless*
joven	*young*
justo/a	*fair*
la lección	*lesson*
el objetivo	*goal*
el paro	*unemployment*
el patio	*playground*
las prácticas	*internship*
profesión	*job, profession*
el/la profesor/a	*teacher*
prohibir	*to prohibit*
el reto	*challenge*
el salario	*salary*
simpático/a	*nice*
suspender	*to fail*
el sueño	*dream*
el trabajo	*job*
la universidad	*university*
útil	*useful*
vago/a	*lazy*

Unit 3 - Foundation vocab building

1. Match up.

Asignatura	Choice
Futuro	School
Curso	Subject
Elección	Goal
Escuela	Money
Objetivo	Job
Carrera	Future
Dinero	Salary
Trabajo	Course
Salario	Career

2. Unscramble and translate.

e.g. eotjbiov: objetivo   goal

a. indeor: ________ ________

b. rrraeac: ________ ________

c. deeebrs: ________ ________

d. euioqp: ________ ________

e ccelóni: ________ ________

f. asgituanra: ________ ________

g. pmresea: ________ ________

h. intlúi: ________ ________

i. xpceilar: ________ ________

3. Gapped translation.

a. Yo busco un trabajo. — *I am looking for a __________.*

b. Yo hago errores. — *I make __________.*

c. Soy malo en matemáticas. — *I am __________ at maths.*

d. Es mi asignatura favorita. — *It is my favourite __________.*

e. Se me dan bien los idiomas. — *I am __________ at languages.*

f. La escuela es aburrida. — *School is __________.*

g. El futuro me asusta. — *The __________ scares me.*

h. La ciencia es difícil. — *Science is __________.*

i. La jornada escolar es larga. — *The __________ day is long.*

j. Los teléfonos están prohibidos. — *Phones are __________.*

4. Spot and correct any wrong English translations.

a. Buscar un trabajo. — *To look for a class.*

b. Hacer un error. — *To make a plan.*

c. Aprender un oficio. — *To learn a skill.*

d. La jornada escolar. — *The journey to school.*

e. Soy malo en matemáticas. — *I am good at maths.*

f. Tengo buenas notas. — *I have good grades.*

g. Mi sueño es viajar. — *My dream is to study.*

h. La física es fascinante. — *Physics is fascinating.*

i. Quiero ser científico. — *I want to be a postman.*

j. El futuro me asusta. — *The future scares me.*

5. Positive (P) or negative (N) opinion?

a. Las matemáticas son difíciles.

b. El inglés es fascinante.

c. La escuela es horrible.

d. Marcos es muy vago.

e. Mi tía es rica y feliz.

f. ¡El profesor García es horrible!

g. La música es inútil.

h. Mi hermano es muy bueno en química.

6. Phrase puzzle: unscramble and translate.

e.g. asignatura favorita mi es: *My favourite subject is*

a. quiero ser llegar yo a policía:

b. un yo trabajo busco:

c. mis de proyectos futuro:

d. encuentro eso yo inútil:

e. es asignatura difícil una:

f. da bien se me el español:

g. dinero ganar espero mucho:

7. Complete the words and translate them.

a. Dif_ _ _ _:

b. Apren_ _ _:

c. Trab_ _ _:

d. Pa_ _ _:

e. Empr_ _ _:

f. Út_ _:

g. Fác_ _:

h. Obj_ _ _ _ _:

i. Hab_ _ _ _ _ _:

j. Exp_ _ _ _ _:

k. Fasc_ _ _ _ _ _:

l. Futu_ _:

m. Prof_ _ _ _ _:

n. Proh_ _ _ _:

8. Tick all the words which refer to money.

a. Asignatura

b. Rico

c. Pobre

d. Útil

e. Joven

f. Salario

g. Difícil

h. Dinero

i. Curso

j. Banco

k. Prácticas

l. Final

9. Complete with the options provided.

a. Yo ___________ un trabajo.

b. Las matemáticas son una ___________ difícil.

c. En el futuro yo seré ___________.

d. El año que viene estudiaré ___________.

e. Después de mis "A-Levels" yo haré unas ______.

f. Yo siempre hago los ___________.

g. Ya no me gusta la escuela. Es ___________.

h. Yo soy bastante ___________ en física.

deberes	malo	prácticas	rica
asignatura	español	aburrida	busco

10. Translate into English.

a. El año que viene estudiaré biología.

b. Busco trabajo en una oficina.

c. Mi sueño es viajar por todo el mundo.

d. Me gustaría tener un trabajo bien pagado.

e. Trabajar en la industria automotriz.

f. Dejaré la escuela después de mis examenes.

g. El futuro me da miedo.

h. Odio las ciencias porque son difíciles.

i. El año que viene quiero estudiar un idioma.

j. No se me dan bien los idiomas.

11. Translate into English.

a. Yo voy a la escuela a pie.

b. Creo que hay demasiados deberes cada noche.

c. El fin de semana pasado jugué al rugby en la escuela.

d. No quiero ir a la universidad.

e. Hay 800 estudiantes en mi escuela.

f. Las clases empiezan a las nueve de la mañana.

g. Fui al teatro con mi clase.

h. En el futuro me gustaría ser abogado.

i. Los uniformes escolares son prácticos.

j. Tengo cinco clases al día.

Unit 3 - Foundation reading

1. **Read these comments from young people about school.**

<table>
<tr><td>

Francisco
Voy andando al colegio. Me gustan las matemáticas, pero no me gusta la historia porque creo que es inútil.

Leila
Creo que hay demasiados deberes, pero me llevo bien con los profesores. Son simpáticos.

Jacinta
En mi opinión, hay demasiadas clases todos los días pero me gusta estar con mis amigos.

</td></tr>
</table>

Who says what? Put a cross in the correct column for each statement.

Who says...	Francisco	Leila	Jacinta
a. There is too much homework.			
b. They like being with their friends.			
c. They get on with the teachers.			
d. There are too many lessons.			
e. They walk to school.			
f. They do not like history.			

2. **Read this online message from Francisco.**

Voy a la escuela en Burgos. Me gustan las clases, pero no los deberes. Tenemos siete clases al día y las clases terminan a las cinco de la tarde. En el recreo hablo con mis amigos en el patio. A la hora de comer, como con los demás alumnos. La comida no me parece muy buena. Me encanta hacer deporte en el colegio porque el profesor no es muy estricto. Es muy simpático.

Complete the gap in each sentence using a word from the box below. There are more words than gaps.

school hall	homework	nice
lessons	strict	playground

a. Francisco does not like ______________.

b. At break he talks with his friends in the ______________.

c. Francisco's PE teacher is ______________.

Unit 3 - Foundation reading

3. Read what these people say about their education.

> **Sandra**
> Creo que las clases son interesantes pero demasiado largas. Además, creo que los profesores hacen bien su trabajo pero nos ponen demasiados deberes.
>
> **Mateo**
> Me llevo muy bien con los profesores y con mis amigos. Las clases me interesan y siempre saco buenas notas.
>
> **Fátima**
> En mi opinión, los profesores son demasiado estrictos y la jornada es demasiado larga para mí. Me gustaría cambiar de colegio.
>
> **Juan Pablo**
> Me interesan las tareas escolares, sobre todo los idiomas. No me gustan todas las normas sobre la ropa y el pelo.

If the person has a positive opinion put P in the box. If they have a negative opinion put N in the box. If they express both a positive and negative opinion put P/N in the box.

Sandra ☐   Mateo ☐   Fátima ☐   Juan Pablo ☐

4. Read what Irene says about one of her teachers.

La profesora se llama señora García. Es profesora de historia y geografía. Es bastante bajita y tiene el pelo corto y castaño. Es bastante estricta, pero también es simpática y me llevo bien con ella. Siempre explica bien la materia.

Entiendo bien sus clases y no pone demasiados deberes. A veces nos habla de su vida privada. Me parece interesante. Creo que es bueno conocer mejor a los profesores.

Tick the three correct statements.

a. Irene's teacher, señora García, teaches history and geography.

b. The teacher is short with long brown hair.

c. The teacher is quite strict but kind.

d. The teacher does not always explain things well.

e. The teacher gives too much homework.

f. Irene likes knowing more about the teacher's personal life.

Unit 3 - Foundation reading

5. Some young people are talking about their future plans. Answer the questions.

> **Isabel**
> En el futuro me gustaría ir a la universidad para estudiar idiomas. Me encanta viajar y conocer a gente nueva.
>
> **Daniela**
> Un día me gustaría trabajar como autora. En el colegio me gustaba mucho leer y escribir cuentos.
>
> **Jorge**
> Mi sueño es ser médico. Sé que es difícil, pero mi madre me anima mucho y voy a trabajar duro.
>
> **Marco**
> No se me dan muy bien las matemáticas, pero soy muy trabajador. Así que en el futuro espero dedicarme a la informática y hacer videojuegos.

a. What subject would Isabel like to study at university?   ______________________________

b. What does she enjoy? Mention two points.   (i) ______________________________

(ii) ______________________________

c. What does Daniela like doing? Mention two points.   (i) ______________________________

(ii) ______________________________

d. What will Jorge do to achieve his career goal?   ______________________________

e. What does Marco want to do? Mention two points.   (i) ______________________________

(ii) ______________________________

6. Daniel writes a message to his Bolivian friend.

En el colegio llevo uniforme. Es práctico, pero no muy cómodo. Además, es bastante caro.

Con respecto a las excursiones escolares, antes no me gustaban, pero ahora me parecen interesantes. El año pasado visitamos un castillo y fue aburrido, pero ayer fuimos al teatro y fue genial. Dentro de quince días iremos a Valencia a visitar el Museo de las Ciencias.

Complete each sentence using a word from the box below. There are more words than gaps.

> | | | | |
> |---|---|---|---|
> | history | uncomfortable | boring | months |
> | great | weeks | inexpensive | school trips |

a. Daniel's uniform is ______________________________.

b. In the past he did not enjoy ______________________________.

c. The visit to the castle was ______________________________.

d. He will visit Valencia in two ______________________________.

Unit 3 - Higher vocabulary building

Vocabulary

a pesar de	*despite*
el abogado	*lawyer*
acosar	*to bully*
aprender	*to learn*
aprobar	*to pass*
la asignatura	*subject*
la carrera	*career, degree*
la confianza	*confidence, trust*
convertirse en	*to become*
los deberes	*homework*
desear	*to wish*
dirigir	*to manage*
duro/a	*hard*
el edificio	*building*
la empresa	*company*
enseñar	*to teach*
la entrevista	*interview*
el equilibrio	*balance*
el equipo	*team*
esperar	*to hope*
estricto/a	*strict*
estudiar	*to study*
el exámen	*exam*
explicar	*to explain*
el futuro	*future*
la habilidad	*skill*
hacer unas prácticas	*do an apprenticeship*
el idioma	*language*
igual	*equal*
joven	*young, young person*
justo/a	*fair*
la lección	*lesson*
inútil	*useless*
el objetivo	*goal*
permitir	*to allow*
práctico/a	*practical*
prohibido/a	*forbidden*
responsable	*responsable*
el sueño	*dream*
el reto	*challenge*
sabático/a	*sabbatical*
sacar buenas/malas notas	*to get good/bad grades*
simpático/a	*nice*
soy bueno/a en	*I'm good at*
soy malo/a en	*I'm bad at*
el trabajo	*job*
traducir	*to translate*
tratar con	*to deal with*
la universidad	*university*
útil	*useful*
vago/a	*lazy*

1. Match up.

Entrevista	Future
Carrera	Job
Equipo	Money
Futuro	Interview
Elección	Salary
Trabajo	To teach
Dinero	Team
Salario	Homework
Deberes	Career
Empresa	To hope
Enseñar	Company
Esperar	Choice

2. Correct the wrong translations.

a. Confianza: *Competence*

b. Entrevista: *Entertaining*

c. Objetivo: *Goal*

d. Acosar: *To bully*

e. Tratar: *To work hard*

f. Reto: *Rat*

g. Trabajo: *Career*

h. Prohibido: *Permitted*

i. Edificio: *It is difficult*

3. One of three: circle the right answers.

Objetivo	*Goal*	*Balance*	*Subject*
Joven	*Old*	*Young*	*Great*
Escuela	*Job*	*School*	*Money*
Trabajo	*Table*	*Screen*	*Job*
Bueno	*Weak*	*Good*	*Strict*
A pesar de	*Despite*	*Also*	*However*
Idioma	*Long*	*Language*	*Sheet*
Horrible	*Great*	*Zero*	*Horrible*
Asignatura	*Subject*	*Job*	*Future*
Sueño	*Dream*	*Worry*	*Hope*
Útil	*Useful*	*Mean*	*Fun*

4. Positive (P) or negative (N)?

a. Ser bueno en

b. Ser malo en

c. Mal pagado

d. Justo

e. Horrible

f. Simpático

g. Vago

h. Bien pagado

i. Útil

5. Complete the translations.

a. Estoy buscando trabajo. *I am looking for a _____________.*

b. Voy a estudiar química. *I am going to study ____________.*

c. Soy malo en matemáticas. *I am ____________ at maths.*

d. Yo aprobé los exámenes. *I ____________ my exams.*

e. Todavía soy joven. *I am still ____________.*

f. Haré un año sabático. *I'll do a sabbatical ____________.*

g. Deseo continuar. *I ____________ to continue.*

h. Me gusta trabajar en equipo. *I like team ____________.*

i. Espero tener éxito. *I ____________ to succeed.*

j. Los idiomas me parecen apasionantes. *I find languages _______.*

k. El acoso escolar es un problema. *____________ is a problem.*

6. Match the opposites.

Justo	Pasado
Bien	Pobre
Horrible	Fácil
Difícil	Injusto
Rico	Desagradable
Útil	Fantástico
Futuro	Trabajador
Agradable	Mal
Vago	Inútil

7. Translate into English.

a. Acosar:

b. Dirigir:

c. Útil:

d. Bien pagado:

e. Trabajo:

f. Difícil:

g. Buscar:

h. Reto:

i. Proyecto:

j. Carrera:

k. Soñar:

l. Habilidad:

m. Éxito:

n. Objetivo:

o. Esperanza:

p. Dinero:

q. Salario:

r. Permitir:

8. Missing letters.

a. D_rigir   *To manage*

b. S_ñar   *To dream*

c. Pr_ctico   *Practical*

d. Din_ro   *Money*

e. Re_o   *Challenge*

f. J_ven   *Young*

g. _rabajo   *Job*

h. Just_   *Fair, just*

i. B_eno   *Good*

9. Unjumble the words and translate.

e.g. maabel: amable   kind

a. bscuar: _________   _________

b. inedro: _________   _________

c. tlúi: _________   _________

d. pranered: _________   _________

e. eqioup: _________   _________

f. dfícili: _________   _________

g. dgriiir: _________   _________

10. Break the flow. Insert lines where there should be gaps.

a. Sufríacosoescolarcuandoerapequeña.

b. Voyatomarmeunañosabáticoen2030.

c. Despuésdelosexámenesbuscarétrabajo.

d. Voyatrabajarenunbancoounaoficina.

e. Esperoganarmuchodinero.

f. Megustaríatrabajarenunatiendaoenunaescuela.

g. Megustaríatrabajarcomoprofesoroabogado.

h. Yosueñoconsermédicoenungranhospital.

11. Complete with the correct verb from the ones in the grid.

a. Yo ____________ como científico.

b. Yo voy a ____________ un año sabático.

c. Yo ____________ dos idiomas.

d. Yo ____________ con hacerme rico.

e. Yo ____________ tener mucho dinero.

f. Yo ____________ un trabajo.

g. Yo voy a ____________ mis exámenes.

h. Me ____________ trabajar como policía.

i. Mis profesores ____________ muy bien.

j. Yo ____________ ser investigador.

k. Yo ____________ profesor.

l. Yo ____________todavía demasiado joven.

estudiaré	**buscaré**	**sueño**
aprobar	**trabajaré**	**espero**
tomarme	**quiero**	**explican**
soy	**gustaría**	**seré**

12. Translate into English.

a. Mis asignaturas favoritas son español y geografía.

b. Siempre me llevo bien con mis profesores.

c. La profesora de matemáticas es estricta, pero amable y trabajadora.

d. Las clases me parecen variadas e interesantes.

e. La profesora de francés explica bien la asignatura.

f. He aprendido mucho visitando el Museo Thyssen.

g. En el recreo charlo con mis amigos en el patio.

h. Quiero ir a la universidad después de los exámenes.

i. Me gustaría hacer un trabajo interesante y bien pagado.

j. Anoche me preparé para mi examen de inglés.

k. La música es más divertida que las matemáticas.

l. Lo que más me gusta es ver a mi mejor amiga.

m. Me gustaría trabajar en el extranjero algún día.

n. Sueño con convertirme en médico/a.

Unit 3 - Higher reading

1. **Read this article about a school in Guatemala, Central America.**

En una escuela primaria de Guatemala suele haber 30 alumnos por clase, pero a menudo los niños no están en clase porque están ayudando a sus padres, que trabajan en los mercados o en el campo.

En 2022 todos los estudiantes de Primaria hicieron un examen para identificar cuánto habían aprendido durante la pandemia de COVID-19. Este examen evaluó los conocimientos de los alumnos en lengua y matemáticas.

En Guatemala, las clases se imparten en español a pesar de que en el país se hablan más de 20 idiomas de origen maya y aproximadamente un 30% de la población habla una de estas lenguas en casa. Por eso, a algunos estudiantes a veces les resulta un poco difícil entender todo lo que se dice en clase y los profesores tienen que traducir los ejercicios en español.

Put a tick next to the three statements made in the article.

a. Children are often absent from school.

b. Parents work in local factories.

c. An exam is taken before secondary school.

d. Lessons are conducted in Spanish.

e. All children speak Spanish with their families.

f. Teachers translate to help the pupils.

2. **Lucas is talking about his plans for the future. Answer the questions in English.**

A mí el futuro me da un poco de miedo, pero sé que quiero viajar por el mundo, quizá estudiar en el extranjero en vez de en Perú. Mi hermano, que es cinco años mayor que yo, está haciendo un año sabático en Inglaterra, donde trabaja como voluntario para una organización benéfica.

Me encantan la música y la lectura, así que me encantaría trabajar en una de esas áreas. No obstante, a veces me pregunto si es sólo un sueño o si podría hacerse realidad. Espero poder encontrar un equilibrio entre lo que me gusta y lo que me permitirá ganarme bien la vida. De momento, intento gestionar todo el trabajo que tengo que hacer para la escuela.

a. How does he feel about the future? _______________________________________

b. Where might he like to study? _______________________________________

c. What is his brother doing? Mention two points. _______________________________________

d. What might he do with his interests? _______________________________________

e. What does he sometimes wonder? _______________________________________

f. What is his current priority? _______________________________________

Unit 3 - Higher reading

3. Josefina is talking about her career plans. Circle the best answer to complete each sentence.

Me llamo Josefina y pronto cumpliré dieciséis años. Cuando tenía trece años, empecé a hacerme preguntas sobre la sociedad actual. En mi opinión, la igualdad entre las personas es lo más importante. Hemos avanzado en materia de seguridad y racismo, pero el sexismo sigue siendo un problema. Las niñas y las mujeres sufren acoso con demasiada frecuencia.

Otro problema es la desigualdad. Los jóvenes sin trabajo tienen sueños, ¡pero poco dinero! Quiero luchar por la igualdad entre las personas. Me gustaría estudiar sobre los derechos de los niños en la universidad y trabajar en el futuro como abogada o periodista.

1.	Josefina will soon be…	a. 15	b. 16	c. 17
2.	The main issue for her is…	a. equality	b. poverty	c. racism
3.	Girls and women are too often…	a. ignored	b. harassed	c. exploited
4.	At university she would like to study…	a. law	b. journalism	c. children's rights
5.	She might become a…	a. lawyer	b. teacher	c. author

4. Read Amira's experience of looking for jobs in Spain. Answer the questions in English.

Encontrar trabajo para una mujer como yo, de nombre árabe, no siempre es fácil. En las entrevistas siempre te sientes menospreciada *(looked down on)* antes incluso de haber tenido la oportunidad de demostrar tus cualidades personales y profesionales. A menudo te dicen que tienes que ser el doble de buena, el doble de cualificada, para tener las mismas oportunidades. Es agotador.

A veces me pregunto si vale la pena seguir luchando. Pero sé que soy fuerte a pesar de los retos. Quiero tener la oportunidad de demostrar que soy capaz. El color de mi piel y mi ropa no deberían importar.

a. How does Amira feel at job interviews?
____

b. What does she find tiring. Mention two points.
____

c. What does she wonder?
____

d. What does she want?
____

e. What does she say in the last sentence?
____

Unit 3 - Higher reading

5. **Read Camilo's description of his school day. Circle the best answer to complete each sentence.**

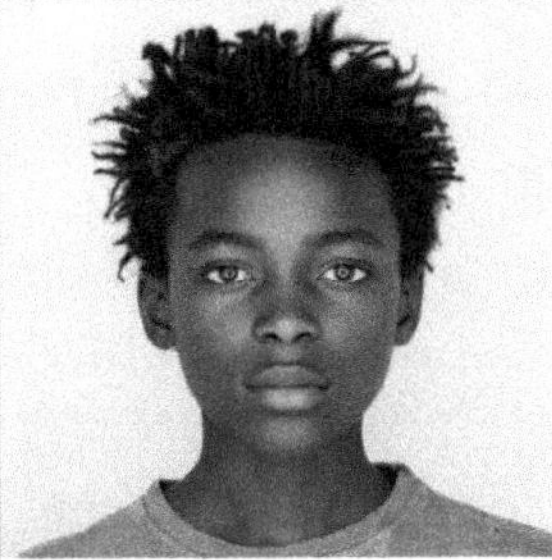

Hoy he tenido un día estupendo. He tenido muchas clases: por la mañana, francés, matemáticas y español. Me gustan las matemáticas, pero español... a mis amigos les parece divertido, pero a mí me aburre un poco y no me llevo bien con el profesor.

Luego he tenido la pausa para comer. Las comidas son sanas, pero también un poco caras y no hay mucha variedad de un día para otro. En la comida charlo con mis amigos lo que siempre es divertido. ¡Hacemos muchas bromas! Los teléfonos móviles están prohibidos, así que no jugamos a ningún videojuego. Además, el patio es demasiado pequeño para jugar al fútbol.

Después de comer tenemos otras clases, como biología y educación física. Historia y geografía son fascinantes porque aprendemos mucho sobre los distintos países del mundo. Eso me interesa.

A las cuatro, por fin termino el día y me voy a casa. No ha sido un día especial, pero aun así lo he pasado bien con mis amigos.

1.	Camilo says his day was...	a. fun	b. pleasant	c. annoying
2.	He finds Spanish lessons...	a. boring	b. enjoyable	c. interesting
3.	School meals are...	a. varied	b. disgusting	c. healthy
4.	At lunchtime with his friends he...	a. has a laugh	b. plays games	c. plays football
5.	After lunch he learned about different...	a. peoples	b. countries	c. languages

6. Read Mireia's description of a school visit. Answer the questions in English.

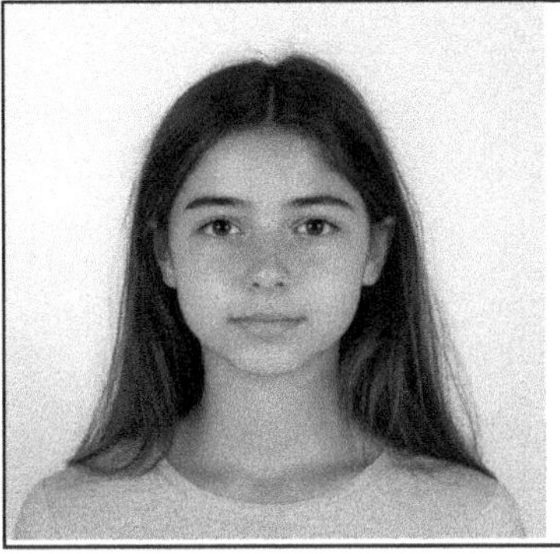

Ayer tuvimos una visita escolar emocionante. Visitamos el Museo de Historia Natural, donde aprendí mucho sobre las especies animales y la historia del planeta. Todo estaba muy bien explicado, tanto en inglés como en español. Nos enseñaron enormes esqueletos de animales. Después de la visita guiada, tuvimos tiempo libre para explorar el museo por nuestra cuenta. Fue un día realmente sorprendente para mí, ya que nunca había visto un museo así.

También pasé un rato con mis amigos, lo que hizo que el día fuera aún más divertido. Volví a casa cansada pero feliz. Estoy deseando vivir más experiencias como ésta en el futuro y crear nuevos recuerdos.

a. How does she describe the day in the first sentence? _______________________________

b. What did she learn about? Mention two points. _______________________________

____

c. What happened after the guided tour? _______________________________

d. Why did she feel surprised? _______________________________

e. What made the day even more fun? _______________________________

f. How did she feel when she got home? _______________________________

Unit 3 - Grammar focus: Simple Future Tense (Regular verbs)

In Unit 2 of the first book of this series, we reviewed the three ways to express the future in Spanish:

- *Mañana **veo** una película con mi amiga.*　　Tomorrow **I watch** a film with my friend.
- *Mañana **voy a ver** una película con mi amiga.*　Tomorrow **I am going to watch** a film with my friend.
- *Mañana **veré** una película con mi amiga.*　　Tomorrow **I will watch** a film with my friend.

PRESENT	NEAR FUTURE	SIMPLE FUTURE TENSE
Yo veo	**Yo voy a ver**	**Yo veré**
(I watch)	*(I am going to watch)*	*(I will watch)*

In Unit 2 of the previous book, we also reviewed the near future tense. Now, we will learn how to conjugate the **simple future tense**, which in English translates to **will + infinitive**.

- El año que viene **estudiaré** en la universidad.　　*Next year I **will study** at university.*
- Mi padre **se jubilará** en dos meses.　　*My father **will retire** in two months.*
- Juan y María **empezarán** a trabajar el mes que viene.　*Juan and María **will start** to work next month.*

To conjugate verbs in the simple future tense, we don't eliminate the ending -AR, -ER or -IR from the verb in infinitive as in other verb conjugations learned in the past. Instead, we add the future endings (highlighted in bold below) to the verb in infinitive: for example, **hablar** + the endings, or **comer** + the endings.

Lastly, we have great news! The endings are the same for all the regular verbs, regardless of whether they end in -AR, -ER or – IR.

Simple future tense of REGULAR AR, ER and IR verbs

HABLAR (to talk)	COMER (to eat)	VIVIR (to live)
Yo hablar**é** (I will talk)	Comer**é**	Vivir**é**
Tú hablar**ás** (you singular will talk)	Comer**ás**	Vivir**ás**
Él/ella/usted hablar**á** (he/she/you formal singular will talk)	Comer**á**	Vivir**á**
Nosotros/as hablar**emos** (we will talk)	Comer**emos**	Vivir**emos**
Vosotros/as hablar**éis** (you plural will talk)	Comer**éis**	Vivir**éis**
Ellos/ellas/ustedes hablar**án** (they/you formal plural will talk)	Comer**án**	Vivir**án**

One last detail: as always, in negative sentences, we write "no" before the conjugated verb:

- El año que viene **no estudiaré** en la universidad.　*Next year I **will not study** at university.*
- Mi padre **no se jubilará** en dos meses.　　*My father **will not retire** in two month.*
- Juan y María **no empezarán** a trabajar.　　*Juan and María **will not start** to work.*

Before moving on to the exercises, do the recognition task below. Look at each verb (all conjugated with "yo") and mark in the box if the verb is in the present tense (PRES), past tense (imperfect, past simple or perfect, all marked as PAST) or in the simple future tense (FUT).

VERB	PRES/PAST/FUT	VERB	PRES/PAST/FUT	VERB	PRES/PAST/FUT
Preferiré		He visitado		Soy	
Prefiero		Visitaré		Era	
He preferido		Jugaba		Seré	
Me gustó		Juego		Estudiaré	
Me gusta		Jugaré		He estudiado	

Now look at the sentences below. They offer other clues about whether the sentence is in the present or past. Look out for **time expressions**, but not every sentence will have one. Mark in the box PRES, PAST, or FUT as you did above.

Normalmente voy andando al colegio.		Ayer hice mis deberes.	
Ayer jugué con mis amigos.		Mañana hablaré con mis amigos.	
Cuando era pequeña hablaba mucho.		El lunes pasado visité un museo.	
Iré al teatro con mi clase.		Las comidas no cambian mucho.	
La profesora explicó muy bien su lección.		Yo iba a la escuela primaria.	
Ahora trabajo en casa.		La profesora explica bien la asignatura.	
Nunca me han gustado las ciencias.		Yo me llevo bien con mis profesores.	
Aprendo mucho en la clase de Música.		He trabajado dos horas. ¡Uf!	
Hace dos años hacía natación.		Nosotros hablaremos mucho en clase.	
El martes que viene jugaré al rugby.		Me encanta estudiar gramática.	

1. Match up.

Bailaré	You (sing.) will talk
Hablarás	You (sing.) will play
Escucharemos	I will eat
Bailarás	You (sing.) will dance
Hablaréis	I will go
Escucharán	I will dance
Escucharé	You (plural) will go
Jugaré	I will play
Iremos	They will listen
Iré	You (plural) will talk
Jugarás	We will go
Iréis	We will listen
Comeré	I will listen

2. Faulty translation: correct the English.

a. Después del colegio iré al parque.
After school you will go to the park.

b. Este verano iremos de vacaciones a España.
This summer they will go on holiday to Spain.

c. Mi primo irá a la universidad el año que viene.
My cousins will go to university next year.

d. Vosotros aprobaréis el examen de física si estudiáis.
We will pass the physics exam if we study.

e. Ellos crearán un robot en la clase de informática.
He will create a robot in computer science class.

f. En el futuro necesitaremos más ingenieros.
In the future, they will need more engineers.

3. Add the missing letters the verbs are either in the present or in the simple future tense.

a. D_ _ _ _ _ _   *We must*

b. E_ _ _ v_   *She goes*

c. V_ _ _ _ _ _   *We will see*

d. Q_ _ _ _ _   *I want*

e. E _ _ _ _ _ _   *He will choose*

f. P_ _ _ _ _ _   *We can*

g. I _ _ _   *You sing. will go*

h. V _ _   *I go*

i. I_ _ _ *They will go*

j. L_ _ _   *They read*

k. ¿Qué h_ _ _ _?   *What are you doing?*

l. A_ _ _ _ _ _ _   *I will learn*

m. S_ _ _ _   *We are*

n. S_ _ _ _ _ _   *We will be*

o. P_ _ _ _ _ _ _   *I prefer*

p. P_ _ _ _ _ _ _ _   *I will prefer*

q. T_ _ _ _ _ _ _   *They work*

r. J _ _ _ _ _   *She will play*

---

4. Insert the right subject pronoun (yo, tú, él, ella, nosotros/as, vosotros/as, ellos, ellas).

a. _______ trabajaremos mucho.

b. A _______ les gustarán las ciencias.

c. _______ comerás en la escuela.

d. ¿Qué estudiaréis _______ en la universidad?

e. _______ deberán llevar uniforme.

f. _______ jugaremos al fútbol.

g. _______ trabajaré por la tarde.

h. A _______ no os gustarán las clases.

i. _______ no irá a la universidad.

j. ¿_______ empezarás a hacer prácticas?

k. _______ organizaremos varias excursiones.

l. _______ irás a la escuela en bicicleta.

m. _______ estudiarán muchas asignaturas.

n. A _______ nos encantará la profesora.

o. _______ continuaré con mis estudios.

p. ¿_______ irá a la escuela en bus?

---

5. Correct the grammar mistakes.

a. Este fin de semana yo hablará con mi primo.

b. Durante el verano mi hermano iré de vacaciones.

c. Mis amigos y yo iréis a la discoteca y bailarás toda la noche.

d. El año que viene tú estudiaréis en la Universidad Complutense de Madrid.

e. Juan no aprobaré el examen de matemáticas porque no ha estudiado.

f. Los profesores irá a un curso de formación en Salamanca.

---

6. Complete with a suitable verb in the simple future tense.

a. Yo es__________ francés este año.

b. Yo ir__________ a la escuela.

c. Ellos ve__________ a sus amigos.

d. Nosotros ju__________ al fútbol.

e. Ellos ap________ matemáticas.

f. Tú tr________ 7 horas al día.

g. Yo ap________ mucho durante el curso.

h. Vosotros es________ química

i. La profesora María en__________ esos cursos.

j. Juan y tú ap__________ el examen de lengua.

Simple future tense of IRREGULAR VERBS

The simple future endings in Spanish are the same for all verbs: **é, ás, á, emos, éis, án**. This is good news :)

However, with irregular verbs we need to use an irregular stem (as opposed to just adding the future ending on to the infinitive):

e.g.	**Regular:**	"hablar"	->	"**hablar**é"	(I will talk)
	Irregular:	"hacer"	->	"**har**é"	(I will do)

<table>
<tr><td colspan="4" align="center">Simple future tense of the most useful IRREGULAR VERBS</td></tr>
<tr><td colspan="2" align="center">HACER (to do/make)</td><td colspan="2" align="center">Other verbs with irregular stems</td></tr>
<tr><td>Yo haré</td><td>I will do</td><td>Decir   to say</td><td>dir-</td></tr>
<tr><td>Tú harás</td><td>you (singular) will do</td><td>Poder to be able to</td><td>podr-</td></tr>
<tr><td>Él/ella/usted hará</td><td>he/she/you (singular formal) will do</td><td>Poner to put</td><td>pondr-</td></tr>
<tr><td rowspan="1">Nosotros/as haremos</td><td>we will do</td><td>Querer to want</td><td>querr-</td></tr>
<tr><td>Vosotros/as haréis</td><td>you (plural) will do</td><td>Saber to know</td><td>sabr-</td></tr>
<tr><td rowspan="1"></td><td></td><td>Salir   to go out</td><td>saldr-</td></tr>
<tr><td>Ellos/ustedes harán</td><td>they/you (formal plural) will do</td><td>Tener to have</td><td>tendr-</td></tr>
</table>

1. Match up.

Podré	You will want
Estudiarás	We will be able to
Aprobarán	You will study
Haré	He will want
Podremos	You will go
Querréis	They will pass
Deberemos	I will be able to
Tendré	I will have
Irás	They will do
Querrá	I will do
Explicaréis	You will explain
Harán	We will have to

2. Faulty translation: correct the English.

a. Después del colegio haré unas prácticas.
After school they will do an apprenticeship.

b. Este verano tendrán que trabajar.
This summer I will have to work.

c. El año que viene estudiaremos en Sevilla.
Next month, we will study in Seville.

d. Mis amigos y yo aprobaremos el examen de inglés.
My friends will pass the English exam.

e. ¿Dónde estudiarás en el futuro?
Where will he study in the future?

f. ¿Por qué no el profesor no enseñará la clase?
Why won't the teachers teach the class?

3. Circle the correct verb conjugation.

a. Yo *saldré/saldrá/tendré* francés en la escuela.

b. Nosotros *estudiaréis/estudiaremos/estudiarán* Literatura.

c. ¿Por qué Juan *querréis/querrá/querrán* hacer esa carrera?

d. Los profesores no *harán/haremos/hará* más exámenes este año.

e. Los estudiantes *organizará/organizarán/organizaré* un seminario.

f. El profesor Javier te *explicarás/explicaré/explicará* muy bien la asignatura.

4. Complete the translation.

a. Yo sa_______________   *I will know.*

b. Tú po_______________   *You will be able to.*

c. Nosotros or__________   *We will organise.*

d. Ellos ex_____________   *They will explain.*

e. Vosotros ha__________   *You will do.*

f. Ellos di_____________   *They will say.*

g. Yo te_______________   *I will have.*

h. Tú en_______________   *You will teach.*

i. Usted qu____________   *You will want.*

j. Yo ap_______________   *I will pass.*

k. Ustedes ir___________   *You will go.*

5. Circle the correct pronoun.

a. *Nosotros/vosotros/ellos* querrán ir a la escuela en coche.

b. *Tú/yo/ella* sabrá las respuestas a las preguntas del profesor.

c. *Nosotros/vosotros/ellos* diremos la verdad.

d. ¿*Ella/tú/nosotros* se lo dirás al profesor?

e. ¿Querrán *ellos/nosotros/tú* participar en el proyecto?

f. ¿Sabrás *ellos/tú/vosotros* llegar a la escuela?

6. Correct the mistakes in the words in italics.

a. Ella *podrás* hacer el examen.

b. Nosotros *iréis* al gimnasio a las cuatro.

c. Mi padre *irás* a la piscina a nadar.

d. Mi hermana no *podré* quedarse después de clase.

e. Mis hermanos *iremos* a la universidad.

f. ¿A qué hora *tendrá* tú que ir a trabajar?

g. ¿*Querrán* vosotros estudiar matemáticas?

h. Yo no *sabrás* responder las preguntas del examen.

7. Present, past or future? Then translate.

Ejemplo: ayer	PAST	yesterday
hoy		
ahora		
el sábado pasado		
el sábado que viene		
hace dos meses		
mañana		
en la actualidad		

8. Circle the correct verb in italics.

a. Ayer yo *voy/fui/iré* a la universidad.

b. En este momento *trabajamos/trabajábamos/trabajaremos* mucho.

c. Marina *juega/jugó/jugará* al fútbol anoche.

d. Mañana, ella *quiere/quiso/querrá* estudiar.

e. Cuando yo *soy/era/seré* joven bailaba.

f. Ahora *escucho/escuché/escuchaba* a la profe bien.

g. *Juego/jugaba/jugaré* al rugby el lunes que viene.

h. Por fin Juan *encuentra/ha encontrado/encontraré* trabajo en Madrid.

9. Complete the translation.

a. Yo __________ mucho — *I work a lot.*

b. Yo __________ Informática — *I will study IT.*

c. Yo ________ feliz en la escuela — *I was happy at school.*

d. Ellos __________ mañana — *They will work tomorrow.*

e. Yo __________ los deberes — *I do the homework.*

f. Ella __________ los deberes — *She did the homework.*

g. Nosotros ____________ un trabajo — *We will find a job.*

10. Present to future: put these present tense verbs in the simple future tense.

e.g. Yo voy   Yo iré

a. Yo trabajo   ____________

b. Tú eres   ____________

c. Él tiene   ____________

d. Nosotros jugamos   ____________

e. Vosotros visitáis   ____________

f. Ellos salen   ____________

11. Answer positively using a whole sentence. Make any changes necessary.

a. ¿Irás mañana a la escuela en coche? Sí, ____

b. ¿Tuviste matemáticas e inglés ayer? Sí, ____

c. ¿Llegarás mañana al colegio a las ocho? Sí, ____

d. ¿Prefieres la química a la física? Sí, ____

e. ¿Has visitado un castillo con tu clase? Sí, ____

f. ¿Irás a la universidad en el futuro? Sí, ____

Unit 3 - Preparing for speaking and writing

1. Complete with the missing letters.

a. Planes para el fu_ _ _ _   *Plans for the future.*

b. Ap_ _ _ _ _ los A-levels   *To pass A-levels.*

c. Yo soy j_ _ _ _   *I am young.*

d. Ella es tr_ _ _ _ _ _ _ _ _   *She is hard-working.*

e. Un año sa_ _ _ _ _ _   *A sabbatical year.*

f. Yo sueño con conver_ _ _me en   *I dream of becoming.*

g. Hoy tu_ _ matemáticas   *I had maths today.*

h. Yo bu_ _ _ _ _ un trabajo   *I will look for a job.*

i. Se m_ d_ bie_ el español   *I am good at Spanish.*

2. Complete the sentences below using one of the verbs below.

a. Yo ___________ un trabajo.

b. Yo ___________ de abogada.

c. Sueño con _________ en médico.

d. Yo __________ a estudiar química.

e. Yo _________ un año sabático.

f. Yo he _________ buenas notas.

sacado	buscaré	convertirme
haré	**voy**	**trabajaré**

3. Complete the Spanish translation.

a. Mi a_______________ favorita es historia.   *My favourite subject is history.*

b. Yo buscaré un t_______________.   *I will look for a job.*

c. Yo haré unas p_______________.   *I will do an apprenticeship.*

d. Yo s_______________ con convertirme en investigador/a.   *I dream of becoming a researcher.*

e. Voy a e_______________ asignaturas científicas.   *I am going to study scientific subjects.*

f. Yo ll_______________ un uniforme negro y blanco.   *I wear a black and white uniform.*

g. Yo h_______________ un año sabático.   *I will do a sabbatical year.*

h. Yo v_________ a trabajar de médico/a.   *I am going to work as a doctor.*

4. Complete the table with the feminine version of the adjectives and nouns below.

Masculino	Femenino
Amable	
Difícil	
Trabajador	
Vago	
Inútil	
Bien pagado	
Actor	
Profesor	
Estricto	
Interesante	
Aburrido	
Fácil	

5. Add the missing accents (if missing) and translate into English.

a. Yo tendre un trabajo bien pagado.

____

b. El año que viene estudiare español.

____

c. Quimica es mi asignatura favorita.

____

d. Sufri acoso escolar de pequeña.

____

e. Yo prefiero las asignaturas cientificas.

____

f. El año que viene hare un año sabatico.

____

6. Complete with the correct option.

a. Actualmente *voy/iba* andando a la escuela.

b. Ayer *saqué/sacaré* buenas notas.

c. El año que viene *terminé/terminaré* mis estudios.

d. En este momento *busco/buscaba* un trabajo.

e. Mañana *aprobaré/aprobé* mi examen.

f. Normalmente no *hago/haré* los deberes.

g. El año pasado *estoy/estaba* en otra clase.

h. En el futuro *soy/seré* rico.

i. Hace dos años yo *trabajaba/trabajaré* demasiado.

7. Complete.

a. Yo busco un t_ _ _ _ _o.

b. Yo hago los d_ _ _ _ _s.

c. Estudio esp_ _ol y fr_ _cés.

d. El año que v_ _ _e.

e. Sueño con c_ _ _ _ _ _ _ _e en médico.

f. Yo hago unas p_ _ _ _ _ _s.

g. Yo seré r_ _o.

h. Yo haré un a_ _ sabá_ _ _ _.

i. Yo he h_ _ _o los deberes.

8. Sentence puzzle: reorder the words to make a correct sentence.

a. Yo un de en ciencias mis aprendo montón clases   *I learn a lot in my science lessons.*

____

b. Yo bien mis con me profesores llevo   *I get on with my teachers.*

____

c. profesor de es demasiado El estricto inglés   *The English teacher is too strict.*

____

d. en con Yo mis hablo amigos el patio   *I chat with my friends on the playground.*

____

e. profesor de explica bien la El asignatura matemáticas *The maths teacher explains the subject well.*

____

9. Translate into Spanish.

a. My favourite subject is Spanish. _______________________________

b. I get on with my teachers. _______________________________

c. The maths teacher is quite strict. _______________________________

d. I think the lessons are fantastic. _______________________________

e. The Spanish teacher explains the subject well. _______________________________

f. I learn a lot in my maths lessons. _______________________________

g. At break I talk with my friends in the playground. _______________________________

h. I dream of going to university. _______________________________

i. I will do an interesting, well-paid job. _______________________________

j. Last night *(Anoche)* I studied for my Spanish exam. _______________________________

k. Music is more fun than maths. _______________________________

l. What I like most is seeing my friends. _______________________________

Unit 3 - Writing and speaking from a photo card

Write something about both of these photos. Write about who you see, where they are and what they are doing. Read out your description.

____

____

____

Answer the following questions related to this topic. Read out your answers.

1. ¿Qué asignaturas prefieres en la escuela? ¿Por qué?

2. Describe tu uniforme escolar. ¿Qué te parece?

3. Háblame un poco de tu rutina escolar.

4. Describe una excursión escolar que has hecho.

5. ¿Qué vas a estudiar el año que viene?

Unit 3 - Speaking in a role-play

Look at the instructions on the left as they would appear in a speaking test. Read aloud with a partner the dialogue on the right. Then do the dialogue a second time, changing the answers or questions in bold. Take turns playing the two roles.

Foundation

1. Say what your favourite school subject is.	1. ¿Cuál es tu asignatura favorita en la escuela? **Música.**
2. Give one opinion about this subject.	2. ¿Por qué la prefieres? **Porque es interesante.**
3. Ask your friend a question about school.	3. ¿Tienes alguna pregunta para mí? **¿Te gusta la escuela?**
4. Say what time your lessons begin.	4. ¿A qué hora comienzan las clases? **A las nueve.**
5. Say what you do after school (give one detail).	5. ¿Qué haces después de las clases? **Hago los deberes.**

Higher

1. Describe a teacher you like (give two details).	1. Háblame de un profesor que te gusta. **Se llama profesora Puri. Es muy amable.**
2. Say what you think about school rules (give one opinion and one reason).	2. ¿Qué piensas de las normas en tu escuela? **Creo que las normas son importantes porque tenemos que garantizar la convivencia.**
3. Ask your friend a question about their future.	3. ¿Tienes alguna pregunta para mí? **¿Qué vas a hacer en el futuro?**
4. Give one advantage and one disadvantage of going to university.	4. ¿Qué opinas de la universidad? **Está bien para tener un buen trabajo en el futuro, pero es un poco cara.**
5. Describe something you did at school yesterday (give one detail).	5. ¿Qué hiciste en la escuela ayer? **Jugué al baloncesto con mis amigos.**

Unit 3 - Foundation writing

Write approximately 50 words in Spanish. Mention all points. Refer to the language in this unit, for example the Foundation Sentence Bank, or do the task in exam conditions, without help. Or do both!

• Your favourite school subject.   • A teacher.   • Sport at school.   • School lunch.   • A future plan.

1. ____

2. ____

3. ____

4. ____

5. ____

Using your knowledge of grammar, complete the sentences below, choosing one of the three options given.

1. Todos los días ___________ a la escuela en bicicleta (ir/voy/vas).

2. Mi asignatura ___________ son las Matemáticas (favorito/favorita/favoritas).

3. En el futuro yo ___________ a la universidad (voy/ir/iré).

4. Nosotros ___________ en español en clase (hablar/hablan/hablamos).

5. El año que viene las clases ___________ a las nueve (comenzaron/comienza/comenzarán).

Foundation/Higher writing

Write approximately 90 words in Spanish. You must refer to each bullet point.

• Homework.   • What you did yesterday at school.   • Plans for the future.

____

____

____

____

____

____

____

Higher writing

Write approximately 150 words about future plans. Cover both bullet points. Refer to the language in this unit, for example the Higher Sentence Bank, or do the task in exam conditions, without help. Or do both!

- The advantages and disadvantages of working in another country.
- Your plans for next year.

Foundation sentence bank

Voy al colegio a pie.	I go to school on foot.
En mi colegio hay 800 alumnos.	There are 800 pupils in my school.
Llevo uniforme, es práctico.	I wear a school uniform; it's practical.
Tengo cinco clases al día.	I have five lessons per day.
Las clases empezarán a las nueve.	Lessons will start at nine o'clock.
Creo que hay demasiados deberes cada tarde.	I think there is too much homework each evening.
Mi asignatura favorita es español.	My favourite subject is Spanish.
Me gusta la historia porque es interesante.	I like history because it is interesting.
El lunes pasado hice una excursión escolar.	Last Monday I did a school trip.
Fui al teatro con mi clase.	I went to the theatre with my class.
El próximo fin de semana jugaré al rugby en el colegio.	Next weekend I will play rugby at school.
En el futuro me gustaría ser abogado.	In the future I would like to become a lawyer.
No quiero ir a la universidad.	I don't want to go to university.
El año que viene estudiaré matemáticas y ciencias.	Next year I will study maths and science.

Higher sentence bank

Mis asignaturas favoritas son español y geografía.	My favourite subjects are Spanish and geography.
Siempre me llevo bien con mis profesores.	I always get on with my teachers.
El profesor de matemáticas es estricto pero amable.	The maths teacher is strict, but kind.
Yo creo que las clases son variadas e interesantes.	I think the lessons are varied and interesting.
La profesora de español explica bien la asignatura.	The Spanish teacher explains the subject well.
Yo aprendí mucho visitando el museo de historia.	I learned a lot visiting the history museum.
En el recreo hablo con mis amigos en el patio.	At break I talk with my friends in the playground.
Yo iré a la universidad.	I will go to university.
Anoche me preparé para el examen de español.	Last night I prepared for my Spanish exam.
La música es más divertida que las matemáticas.	Music is more fun than maths.
Lo que más me gusta es ver a mis amigas.	What I like most is seeing my friends.
Trabajaré en el extranjero algún día.	I will work abroad one day.
Podría ser médico o profesor.	I could be a doctor or a teacher.
Me gustaría hacer un trabajo interesante y bien pagado.	I would like to do an interesting, well-paid job.

UNIT 4

Travel and tourism

Contents

- Foundation vocab building
- Foundation reading
- Higher vocab building
- Higher reading
- Grammar focus: adverbs
- Preparing for speaking and writing
- Writing and speaking from a photo card
- Speaking in a role play
- Writing
- Sentence banks

Unit 4 - Foundation vocab building

Vocabulary

acordarse	to remember
el aeropuerto	airport
el alojamiento	accommodation
alquilar	to rent
el autocar	coach
el avión	plane
el barco	boat
la bicicleta/bici	bicycle
el billete	ticket
el bosque	forest
la calma	quiet, calm
el camping	camping, campsite
el campo	countryside
caro/a	expensive
el clima	climate
el coche	car
la cocina	kitchen, cuisine
cocinar	to cook
la costa	coast
costar	to cost
descansar	to rest
descubrir	to discover
la estación	station
extranjero/a	foreign
ir al extranjero	to go abroad
fuera	outside
la isla	island
limpio/a	clean
el lugar	place
la maleta	suitcase
el mar	sea
la montaña	mountain
la orilla del mar	seashore
el país	country
pasar	to spend (time)
la playa	beach
quedarse	to stay
rápidamente	quickly
rápido/a	fast
el recuerdo	souvenir, memory
reservar	to book
salir	to leave
seguro/a	safe
el tiempo	weather
el turismo	tourism
viajar	to travel
el viaje	journey
viejo/a	old (mostly objects)
visitar	to visit
la vista	view
volar	to fly
el vuelo	flight

1. Match up.

Lugar	Forest
País	To stay
Orilla	Ticket
Playa	Seashore
Quedarse	Clean
Bosque	Beach
Salir	Weather
Limpio	Place
Tiempo	Sea
Mar	To leave
Billete	Country

2. Correct the incorrect translations.

a. Bebidas frías: *Cold food.*

b. Hacía calor: *It was windy.*

c. En el extranjero: *At home.*

d. Una isla desierta: *A desert island.*

e. Lugares bonitos: *Ugly places.*

f. Playas limpias: *Clean beaches.*

g. Alojamiento: *Means of transport.*

h. Perder una maleta: *To lose money.*

i. Un billete de avión: *A plane ticket.*

3. One of three: circle the right answer.

Maleta	Means	Suitcase	Flight
Mar	Mother	Coast	Sea
Playa	Plague	Suitcase	Beach
Avión	Boat	Plane	Bus
Alquilar	To sell	To buy	To rent
Salir	To leave	To visit	To spend
Extranjero	Foreign	Outside	Safe
Lugares	Beaches	Places	Towns
Comprar	To sell	To travel	To buy
Volar	To fly	Flight	Plane

4. Tick the words to do with transport.

a. Volar

b. Coche

c. Autobús

d. Tiempo

e. Playa

f. Bicicleta

g. Avión

h. Bosque

5. Complete the translation.

a. Un viaje largo: A long ______________.

b. Descubrir lugares históricos: To ______________ historic places.

c. Comprar recuerdos: To ______________ souvenirs.

d. Nadar en el mar: To ______________ in the sea.

e. Descansar en la piscina: To ______________ at the pool.

f. Viajar en avión: To travel by ______________.

6. Translate into English.

a. Rápidamente

b. Vista

c. Tiempo

d. Pasar tiempo

e. Lugares

f. Vuelo

g. Quedarse

h. Playa

i. Calor

j. Limpio

k. País

l. Extranjero

7. Sentence puzzle – put the words in each sentence in the right order.

a. playas Había bonitas   *There were beautiful beaches.*
____

b. bonito Era y mucho hacía calor   *It was beautiful and very hot.*
____

c. Nosotros en bonito un nos quedamos en la hotel costa   *We stayed in a beautiful hotel on the coast.*
____

d. vuelo El París fue agradable a corto y   *The flight to Paris was short and pleasant.*
____

e. el En pueblo un montón ruido de había   *In the town there was a lot of noise.*
____

f. región llena de lugares históricos La estaba   *The region was full of historic places.*
____

h. Marruecos El pasado pasamos nuestras año vacaciones en   *Last year we spent our holidays in Morocco.*
____

---

8. Complete with the correct option.

a. Hace _____________.

b. La isla era muy _____________.

c. He visitado el _____________ de España.

d. Nosotros _____________ en coche.

e. Nos alojaremos en un __________ de lujo.

f. Hay varios __________ históricos que se pueden visitar.

g. Las vistas eran _____________.

h. Yo _____________ el mar a la montaña.

lugares
bonita
prefiero
sur
hotel
viajamos
calor
fantásticas

---

9. Translate into English.

a. Yo salí el catorce de julio.

b. Llegué el quince de julio.

c. Viajé en barco.

d. El viaje fue aburrido.

e. Me alojé en un hotel en la costa.

f. Nadaba todos los días.

---

10. Tick all the geographical terms.

a. Montaña

b. Cocina

c. Norte

d. Sur

e. Río

f. Maleta

g. Bosque

h. Avión

i. Región

j. País

k. Mar

---

11. Translate into English.

a. Me gusta coger el tren y el avión pero prefiero el coche.

b. Desafortunadamente, viajar en avión es malo para el medio ambiente.

c. Fui a la playa en coche con mis padres.

d. Necesitas un coche en el campo.

e. Hay tiendas, hoteles y restaurantes cerca de nuestro camping.

f. El año pasado fui a Francia en coche y en barco.

g. El próximo verano me quedaré en Inglaterra durante las vacaciones.

h. Me gustan las vacaciones junto al mar porque me encanta la playa.

i. Durante las vacaciones compré algunos recuerdos para mis amigos.

j. Me gusta el campo porque es tranquilo y bonito.

k. Prefiero las vacaciones en el extranjero porque son más interesantes.

Unit 4 - Foundation reading

1. **Read what these young people say about transport.**

> **Lisa**
> Me encanta tomar el tren. Es una forma rápida de desplazarse. Además, hay una estación cerca de mi casa.
>
> **Sara**
> Me encanta volar para hacer viajes largos. Sin embargo, sé que volar no es bueno para el clima. Eso me preocupa.
>
> **Francisco**
> Suelo viajar mucho en coche. Es estupendo porque puedo viajar adonde quiera y cuando quiera.

Who says what? Put a cross in the correct column for each question.

Who…	Lisa	Sara	Francisco
a. …travels a lot by car?			
b. …travels by plane?			
c. …likes taking the train?			
d. …worries about the environment?			
e. …can travel when they want?			
f. …has a train station nearby?			

2. **Read what Juan Marcos says about travel in his city.**

El transporte público de mi ciudad suele ser rápido y puntual. Todos los días cojo el tren para ir a trabajar. El trayecto dura veinte minutos y luego tengo que caminar cinco minutos.

Además, todos los fines de semana mis amigos y yo vamos en coche a la playa. El aeropuerto está a treinta minutos de mi casa pero preferimos no volar.

Complete each sentence using a word from the box below. There are more words than gaps.

> cycles   beach   car   late
> mountains   plane   fast   walks

a. Juan Marcos says public transport is _______________

b. To get to work he also takes the train and _______________

c. At the weekend he goes to the _______________

d. He prefers not to travel by _______________

Unit 4 - Foundation reading

3.   Read what these people think about cars.

Pedro

Con un coche, puedes salir de casa y viajar a donde quieras inmediatamente. Me parece muy práctico.

Adel

Cuando vives en una gran ciudad, no necesitas un coche muy grande. Lo prefiero así porque el transporte público contamina menos. No obstante, sé que los coches grandes son prácticos para los viajes largos.

Vega

Vendí mi coche porque era demasiado caro. Ahora voy al trabajo en bicicleta. Es más barato y sano.

Montserrat

Voy a comprarme un coche eléctrico. Son rápidos y limpios. Es bueno para el medio ambiente.

If the person has a positive opinion about cars put P in the box. If they have a negative opinion put N in the box. If they express both a positive and negative opinion put P/N in the box.

Pedro [ ]   Adel [ ]   Vega [ ]   Montserrat [ ]

4.   Three people are giving their opinion about holidays.

Mercedes

En mi opinión, hay que irse regularmente de vacaciones. Es bueno para la salud cuando se trabaja mucho todo el tiempo.

Víctor

Ir de vacaciones no es sencillo para todos. Algunas personas no se lo pueden permitir porque tienen demasiados gastos o poco dinero.

Lidia

Prefiero ir de vacaciones al extranjero. Me encanta conocer otros países y hablar otro idioma. Es muy divertido.

Circle the correct answer in each case.

1. Mercedes thinks holiday are good for...   (a) sightseeing   (b) families   (c) health

2. Víctor talks about...   (a) cost   (b) environment   (c) work

3. Lidia likes holidays...   (a) by the sea   (b) abroad   (c) in France

Unit 4 - Foundation reading

5. **Read Silvia's comment about tourism in her region. Then answer the questions in English.**

Creo que el turismo en los Pirineos catalanes tiene ventajas e inconvenientes.

Los turistas crean puestos de trabajo para la población local. Comen en nuestros restaurantes y utilizan nuestros hoteles y alojamientos.

Pero el turismo de masas es malo para el medio ambiente. Por ejemplo, algunos deportes de invierno tienen un impacto negativo sobre los bosques. Es una pena.

a. What does Silvia first say about tourism? ______________________________________

b. Why does she refer to local people? ______________________________________

c. What do tourists do? Mention two points. ______________________________________

d. What environmental impact does she mention? ______________________________________

6. **Read this extract from a tourist brochure about Frías, Burgos, Spain.**

Este es un pueblo antiguo. Tenemos un parque natural y a todos les encanta el castillo histórico. No hay un supermercado grande, pero sí hay una tienda de comestibles, cafeterías y tiendas donde los visitantes pueden comprar regalos para recordar sus vacaciones. A la gente le encanta montar en bicicleta aquí.

Circle the correct answer in each case.

1. The village is...	(a) small	(b) old	(c) beautiful
2. There are...	(a) supermarkets	(b) gift shops	(c) hotels
3. People enjoy...	(a) cycling	(b) walking	(c) boating

7. **Read this description of a popular tourist destination in Cuba, a Spanish speaking island in the Caribbean.**

El pueblo de Viñales está situado en la provincia de Pinar del Río, Cuba, al oeste de la isla. Es famoso por su impresionante paisaje natural y sus campos de tabaco. Puedes comer en restaurantes, pasar una semana en una casa con vistas a la sierra y dar paseos por el campo o por la montaña. La ciudad más grande de Cuba, La Habana, está a unas tres horas en coche.

a. Where exactly is Viñales? Mention two points. ______________________________________

b. What is it famous for? Mention two points. ______________________________________

c. Where can you go for a walk? Mention two points. ______________________________________

d. What is said about the biggest city? ______________________________________

Unit 4 - Higher vocabulary building

Vocabulary

abierto/a	open
acordarse	to remember
el aeropuerto	airport
el alojamiento	accommodation
alrededor (de)	around
apreciar	to appreciate
el autocar	coach
el barco	boat
la bicicleta/bici	bicycle
el billete	ticket
el bosque	forest
la calma	quiet, calm
el campo	countryside
el clima	climate
la cocina	kitchen, cuisine
costar	to cost
descubrir	to discover
disfrutar	to enjoy
el edificio	building
la estancia	stay
estrecho/a	narrow
extranjero/a	foreign
ir al extranjero	to go abroad
fuera	outside
la isla	island
la lluvia	rain
el lugar	place
la maleta	suitcase
el mar	sea
nadar	swim
numeroso/a	numerous
la orilla del mar	seashore
el país	country
el paisaje	landscape
pasar	to spend (time)
perder	to miss
la playa	beach
quedarse	to stay
rápidamente	quickly, fast
el recuerdo	souvenir, memory
reservar	to book
el río	river
seguro/a	safe
sorprender	to surprise
el tiempo	weather
el tráfico	traffic
el turismo	tourism
las vacaciones	holiday(s)
viajar	to travel
el viaje	journey
la vista	view
volar	to fly
el vuelo	flight

1. Match up.

Costa	Flight
Mar	Ticket
Lugar	Island
Vuelo	Coast
Billete	Stay
Delfín	Rain
Isla	Plane
Avión	Sea
Estancia	Meal
Vista	Dolphin
Comida	Place
Lluvia	Wind
Viento	View

2. Correct the wrong English translations.

a. En la orilla: *On the seabed.*

b. Un país extranjero: *A foreign Paris.*

c. Salir de noche: *To sleep at night.*

d. Un lugar bonito: *A beautiful object.*

e. Cruzar el mar: *To cross the river.*

f. Soñar con…: *To think about...*

g. Un hotel caro: *A cheap hotel.*

h. Una isla española: *A Spanish city.*

i. Un delfín en el mar: *A crab in the sea.*

3. One of three: circle the correct answers.

Fuera	Inside	Outside	Beyond
Lugar	Lake	Place	Town
Costar	To pay	To buy	To cost
Lluvia	Snow	Rain	Sun
País	Region	Country	City
Estancia	Stay	Place	Rest
Tiempo	Weather	Rain	Climate
Estrecho	Long	Wide	Narrow
Vista	Young	View	Old
Vuelo	River	Flight	Journey
Pasar	To go	To buy	To spend

4. Spot and translate the verbs on the list below.

a. Río

b. Salir

c. Traducir

d. Extranjero

e. Sorprender

f. Limpio

g. Perder

h. Descubrir

5. Complete the translations.

a. El paisaje es muy bonito. *The _________ is very beautiful.*

b. Nosotros fuimos al extranjero. *We went ___________.*

c. Disfruté de mis vacaciones. *I _______________ my holidays.*

d. Lo mejor fue… *The _____________ thing was…*

e. El vuelo fue largo. *The _________ was long.*

f. Las tiendas estaban abiertas. *The shops were ___________.*

g. Las playas estaban limpias. *The beaches were ____________.*

h. Elegimos un hotel bonito. *We _________ a beautiful hotel.*

i. La isla era muy tranquila. *The ____________ was very quiet.*

j. Las vistas fueron increíbles. *The ____________ was amazing.*

k. Nuestra estancia fue corta. *Our _________ was short.*

6. Match the opposites.

Caro	Malo
Comprar	Largo
Bueno	Barato
Frío	Aburrirse
Salir	Encontrar
Corto	Vender
Divertirse	Sucio
Limpio	Calor
Perder	Llegar

7. Circle the correct option.

a. Yo *pasé/pasó/pasaste* bien las vacaciones.

b. Yo *viajé/pasé/compré* algunos recuerdos.

c. *Hizo/salió/pasó* buen tiempo.

d. *Llegué/elegí/me quedé* un buen hotel

e. El viaje *fui/fuiste/fue* largo y aburrido.

f. *Desayunó/salió/almorzó* todas las noches.

g. Yo *jugué/perdí/pasé* mi maleta.

h. Tú *fuiste/viajaste/compraste* muchas cosas.

i. Anteayer *compré/toqué/fui* a la playa.

8. Missing letters.

a. Cal_r — *Hot*

b. Pa_s — *Country*

c. H_tel — *Hotel*

d. V_sta — *View*

e. Co_ta — *Coast*

f. R_o — *River*

g. Cor_o — *Short*

h. Pla_a — *Beach*

I. Com_das — *Meals*

9. Break the flow. Insert lines where there should be gaps.

a. LaisladeCubatieneunahistoriamuyinteresante.

b. ElegimosunhoteldelujofrentealmarenSanSebastián.

c. Puderelajarmeydescansarenlaplaya.

d. Hizobuentiempocasitodoslosdías,peroundíallovió.

e. NosfuimosdevacacionesalasmontañasdeChile.

f. Viajamosenaviónyluegoalquilamosuncochepequeño.

g. Lopeorfueeltiempoporquehizofríotodoslosdías.

h. Eldíafuecortoperoagradableporquedescansébien.

10. Unjumble the words and translate.

e.g. entvio: viento   *wind*

a. obntio: _______ _______

b. ocar: _______ _______

c. furae: _______ _______

d. arm: _______ _______

e. ienve: _______ _______

f. erdper: _______ _______

g. slia: _______ _______

11. Complete with the correct verb from the ones in the grid.

a. Yo _______ en avión.

b. Yo _______ en una discoteca.

c. Yo _______ algunos lugares increíbles.

d. _______ buen tiempo.

e. Yo _______ un hotel muy bonito.

f. Yo _______ mi maleta.

g. Yo perdí y _______ mi pasaporte.

h. Yo _______ en el mar.

i. Yo _______ varios recuerdos.

j. Yo me _______ en la playa

k. Yo fui a _______ todas las noches.

l. Yo no _______ alcohol.

bebí	**hizo**	**perdí**	**elegí**
descubrí	**compré**	**bailé**	**bailar**
encontré	**viajé**	**relajé**	**nadé**

12. Translate into English.

a. Los trenes son más limpios que los aviones.

b. Me encanta viajar en tren porque es muy rápido.

c. Ir en bicicleta es mejor para la salud.

d. A pesar de la contaminación, el coche es práctico.

e. El transporte público es rápido y puntual.

f. Caminé mucho cuando fui a España.

g. Puedes caminar por las montañas.

h. Pienso quedarme en Inglaterra este año.

i. Había una vista del mar muy bonita.

j. Descubrí pequeñas calles y restaurantes.

k. Espero volver a Francia el año que viene.

l. Lo que más me gusta es el clima.

m. Me gustaría ir a Australia algún día.

n. Nunca olvidaré estas vacaciones.

o. Nos alojamos en un hotel junto al mar.

Unit 4 - Higher reading

1. Read this article about a museum in Pascua, a Chilean island in the Pacific Ocean.

Reabierto en 2011, el museo de Rapa Nui abrió sus puertas por primera vez en 1973 y es una visita popular entre los turistas. El museo conserva y explica la historia y cultura de la isla de Pascua y de sus habitantes originarios, los rapa nui. Dentro del museo, puedes encontrar objetos arqueológicos, pinturas y fotografías relacionadas con la cultura rapa nui. La entrada es gratuita y el museo está abierto de lunes a viernes, de nueve de la mañana a cinco de la tarde, y los sábados de nueve a doce y media.

    a.   When did the museum first open?   _________________________________

    b.   What two things is the museum about?   _________________________________

    c.   What three types of objects can you find in the museum?

        ____

    d.   When is the museum open?   _________________________________

2. Read Leila's message to a friend.

Creo que las vacaciones son importantes porque necesito descansar después de meses de trabajo. En este momento estoy junto al mar, con el móvil en una mano y un helado en la otra. Hace seis meses, practicaba deportes de invierno en los Pirineos. Antes fui a los castillos que hay en Cataluña y pronto me quedaré con mi tía en Sevilla.

Write P for something that happened in the past, N for something that is happening now, F for something that will happen in the future. Write the correct letter in each box.

a) Visiting castles. ☐   c) Sitting on a beach. ☐

b) Visiting an aunt. ☐   d) Doing winter sports. ☐

3. Read what Ricardo says about his Easter holiday, then circle the best options and answer the question.

En Semana Santa fui a Logroño, en La Rioja, con mi familia. Visitamos el gran mercado del domingo, donde compramos productos locales y donde también vi una camiseta muy chula. No la compré porque costaba cuarenta euros. Después, mi hermano y yo fuimos de compras por la calle principal y luego alquilamos un patinete eléctrico y fuimos a un restaurante.

Tengo que admitir que me encantó esta ciudad porque había mucho que hacer. Además, cuando fuimos hacía un tiempo estupendo, y al atardecer, la vista era muy bonita con la puesta de sol.

    1.   On what day was there a market? a) Friday   b) Sunday   c) Every day

    2.   At the market Ricardo bought: a) Local products   b) Clothes   c) Seafood

    3.   They went to the restaurant... a) On foot   b) By scooter   c) Taxi

    4.   How would you translate the term "puesta de sol"? ___________________________

Unit 4 - Higher reading

4. Read this article about tourist destinations in Quito, Ecuador.

> **El centro histórico**
>
> Sin duda, debes visitar el centro histórico y ver sus monumentos y edificios históricos, como la catedral o el Palacio Municipal. También puedes pasear por sus calles estrechas, descansar en sus jardines y parques y disfrutar de la cocina local.
>
> **El parque Itchimbía**
>
> En el parque Itchimbía podrás disfrutar de unas vistas excelentes de la ciudad. También podrás hacerte una foto con el famoso letrero de "Quito" y visitar el Palacio de Cristal, que ahora es un centro cultural. ¡Disfruta de la naturaleza de Quito en este parque!
>
> **Barrio La Mariscal**
>
> Regálate una noche que no olvidarás en este barrio, el más moderno y con *más fiesta de Quito. No dudes en cenar aquí porque algunos de los mejores restaurantes de Quito están en este barrio. Por último, una parada imprescindible en esta zona es el Mercado Artesanal La Mariscal, donde podrás comprar productos artesanos y locales y hablar con los vendedores.
>
> *This is a synonym of 'el más animado' – *the most lively*

    a.   What is said about the streets in the historical centre? ____________________________

    b.   Where can you rest in the city centre? ____________________________

    c.   What can visitors do in Itchimbía? Mention two details. ______________________

    d.   How is the neighbourhood of La Mariscal described? ______________________

    e.   What can you do with the shop sellers in La Mariscal? ______________________

    f.   How would you translate "artesano"? ____________________________

5. Read what Muriel says about her holiday in Galicia, Spain.

> Durante una semana, tuve la oportunidad de descubrir Galicia, mi región favorita de España. Mis vacaciones empezaron con un viaje en tren, que me permitió admirar los paisajes del norte del país. Nuestro alojamiento en Galicia era una casa de campo de dos plantas con campos alrededor.
>
> Durante mi estancia, exploré las ciudades pesqueras y los mercados de productos locales. Descubrí pequeños restaurantes de pescado y marisco fresco. Además, un día visité un castillo y después, di un largo paseo en bicicleta. Me sorprendió que no lloviera. Nunca olvidaré esas vacaciones.

    a.   What did she do during her train journey? ____________________________

    b.   What was the house like? Mention two details. ____________________________

    c.   What restaurants did she find? Mention two details. ______________________

    d.   When did she do the bike ride? ____________________________

    e.   What surprised her? ____________________________

Unit 4 - Higher reading

6. Read this article about tourism in Granada, Spain.

Granada, una hermosa región de España, recibe cada año la visita de numerosos turistas. Situada al sur de España, la región ofrece actividades para todos los gustos. Puedes descubrir su cultura y arquitectura, como la Alhambra, un palacio de origen musulmán.

En verano, hace calor y puedes disfrutar de las playas de Granada y dar un paseo por las montañas, que ofrecen unas vistas fantásticas. En invierno, hace frío y las montañas de Sierra Nevada tienen mucha nieve. Por eso, los deportes de invierno son muy populares en esta época del año.

En resumen, en Granada puedes vivir experiencias únicas y apreciar la belleza natural y riqueza cultural de la región a lo largo de todo el año.

    a.   Where is the region of Granada?

    b.   Mention two things you can do in the summer.

    c.   How would you translate the word *dar un paseo*?

    d.   What is said about the weather in summer and winter?

    e.   According to the last sentence, what can visitors enjoy? Mention two details.

7. Read this advert for a holiday home in Argentina.

Piso en venta en un pequeño edificio antiguo en las afueras de San Carlos de Bariloche. En el tercer piso con vistas a la montaña. Mucho espacio, con cuatro habitaciones, pero atención, el piso necesita ser renovado.

Ideal para una familia pequeña. Panadería, tienda de comestibles y farmacia a 200 metros. Estación de tren a 20 minutos en coche.

Vendemos este piso por el fallecimiento de nuestros abuelos.

    a.   Where is the apartment? Mention three details.

    b.   What should buyers keep in mind?

    c.   Who would suit this apartment?

    d.   Why is the apartment being sold?

Unit 4 - Grammar focus: adverbs

An **adverb** is a word that usually **qualifies a verb**, meaning it provides additional information about how, where or when something occurs. For example, in the sentence: "He ate his breakfast **quickly**", the word "**quickly**" is an **adverb** because it tells us how he ate (the verb) his breakfast. **Adverbs** sometimes **qualify** other words, for example "**very**" is an **adverb** which **qualifies an adjective**, as in "very good".

Forming adverbs from -o ending adjectives

Very often adverbs are formed from adjectives. To turn adjectives that have a masculine and feminine form (such as rápido/rápida) into adverbs, choose the feminine form and then add *-mente*. Adding **-mente** is the equivalent of adding *-ly* in English (quick-**ly**). Below you can see how to get from an adjective to an adverb using this process.

Rápid**o** (masc. form- adjective) - - -> Rápid**a** (fem. form- adjective) - - -> Rápida**mente** (adverb)

- Él es **rápido**   *He is **quick***   (adjective)
- Él corre **rápidamente**   *He runs **quickly***   (adverb)

Adverbial agreement

Unlike adjectives, adverbs do not agree in gender or number with the nouns they modify.

- Él/ella corre **lentamente**   *He runs **slowly***
- Ellos/ellas corren **lentamente**   *They run **slowly***

Key adjectives that become adverbs by adding -mente

Adjective		Adverb	
Actual	*Current*	**Actualmente**	*Currently*
Fácil	*Easy*	**Fácilmente**	*Easily*
General	*General*	**Generalmente**	*Generally*
Grave	*Serious*	**Gravemente**	*Seriously*
Igual	*Equal*	**Igualmente**	*Equally, also*
Lenta	*Slow*	**Lentamente**	*Slowly*
Rápida	*Quick*	**Rápidamente**	*Quickly*
Tranquila	*Quiet, calm*	**Tranquilamente**	*Quietly*
Triste	*Sad*	**Tristemente**	*Sadly*

Other key adverbs

Many adverbs do not follow this pattern, as they are not linked to an adjective in this way or don't follow the rule above. Below is a list of common adverbs and adverbial phrases in the GCSE Spanish word lists.

Bien (well)	**Mal** (badly)	**Mejor** (better)	**Peor** (worse)	**Quizás, tal vez** (maybe)	**Despacio** (slowly)	**Deprisa** (quickly)
Hoy (today)	**Ahora** (now)	**Mañana** (tomorrow)	**Ayer** (yesterday)	**Antes** (before)	**Después** (after)	**Luego** (later)
Pronto (soon)	**A veces** (sometimes)	**Siempre** (always)	**Nunca** (never)	**Ya** (already)	**Todavía** (still, yet)	**Incluso** (even)
Aquí/acá (here)	**Allí/allá** (there)	**Cerca** (close)	**Lejos** (far)	**Dentro** (inside)	**Fuera** (far)	**Alrededor** (around)
Mucho (a lot)	**Muy** (very)	**Todo** (all)	**Demasiado** (too much/many)	**Poco** (not much)	**Bastante** (quite)	**Nada** (nothing)

Some adverbs, such as those used to express spatial relationships, like "cerca", "lejos", and time, "antes" and "después" can be followed by the preposition "de"(of, to, from):

- Está cerca/lejos **de** aquí   *It is near/far from here*
- Después **de** comer, me gusta dar un paseo   *After eating, I like to go for a walk*

Spot the adverbs

In the sentences below underline any words or groups of words which are adverbs. Find them and translate them into English. Careful! There may be more than you think!

a. Reciclo regularmente los residuos.	g. Afortunadamente hay muchas tiendas pequeñas.
b. Ahora estoy en la estación con mis amigos.	h. Solemos ir a la ciudad mucho.
c. He llegado tarde al colegio.	i. El apartamento está bastante lejos.
d. La iglesia está allí, enfrente del mercado.	j. La Alhambra está muy bien conservada.
e. Hay demasiadas tiendas aquí en San Telmo.	k. Mañana iré a París en tren a las diez.
f. A menudo visitamos el mercado antiguo.	l. Tal vez iremos a visitar el castillo.

1. Match up: time adverbs.

A menudo	Never
Siempre	Late
Nunca	Often
A veces	After
Tarde	Always
Bastante	Sometimes
Pronto	Yesterday
Entonces	Quite
Recientemente	Before
Mañana	Early
Ayer	Then
Ahora	Recently
Antes	Tomorrow
Después	Now

2. Complete with a suitable adverb.

a. H__________ he tomado el autobús para ir a la ciudad.

b. S__________ voy a la ciudad en bicicleta.

c. A __________ prefiero viajar en avión.

d. N__________ vuelo para proteger el planeta.

e. Hicimos las maletas y d__________ fuimos al aeropuerto.

f. A__________ de visitar el museo compré las entradas por internet.

g. La playa está c__________ del pueblo.

h. Llegamos muy p__________ para el vuelo.

i. Nos vamos m__________ de vacaciones al extranjero.

j. Debido al tráfico, llegué a la estación t__________.

k. T__________ no he reservado mis billetes de avión.

3. Adverbs from adjectives: complete the list.

a. Actual: actualmente

b. Rápida: __________________

c. Reciente: _______________

d. Fácil: __________________

e. General: ________________

f. Normal: ________________

g. Lenta: _________________

h. Abierta: ________________

i. Regular: ________________

j. Directa: __________________

k. Completa: ________________

l. Probable: ________________

m. Falsa: _________________

n. Absoluta: ________________

o. Extremada: ______________

p. Afortunada: ______________

q. Cierta: _________________

r. Final: _________________

4. Translate into English.

a. Bien __________

b. Mejor __________

c. Mal __________

d. Peor __________

e. Todavía __________

f. Ya __________

g. Incluso __________

h. Después __________

i. Cerca __________

5. Add the missing letters.

a. L__t________ — *Slowly*

b. __c_lm___e — *Easily*

c. _i_mpr_ — *Always*

d. _ v_c__ — *Sometimes*

e. _h_r_ — *Now*

f. A__e_ — *Before*

g. __ y — *Today*

h. _y__ — *Yesterday*

i. _nc___o — *Even*

j. R_ci___e______ — *Recently*

k. A m__u_o — *Often*

l. P__nt_ — *Soon*

m. M__ — *Very*

n. __n _a — *Never*

o. C__c_ — *Close*

p. M__a_a — *Tomorrow*

q. D_p_i__ — *Quickly*

r. M__o_ — *Better*

6. Add the vowels and translate.

a. G_n_r_l_m_nt_: ______________

b. _bs_l_t_m_nt_: ______________

c. R_l_t_v_m_nt_: ______________

d. _xtr_m_d_m_nt_: ______________

e. R__lm_nt_: ______________

f. _ ct__lm_nt_: ______________

g. P_rf_ct_m_nt_: ______________

h. _f_rt_n_d_m_nt_: ______________

i. C__rt_m_nt_: ______________

7. Translate into Spanish.

a. Yesterday ___________	f. Before ___________	k. Always ___________
b. Tomorrow ___________	g. Already ___________	l. Better ___________
c. Sometimes ___________	h. There ___________	m. Worse ___________
d. After ___________	i. Here ___________	n. Fast ___________
e. Now ___________	j. Then ___________	o. Recently ___________

8. How, where or when? Circle the only possible answer.

a. ¿Cuándo vas a las islas Galápagos?   Mañana/Ayer/Todavía

b. ¿Cómo llegaron a Londres?   Ayer/Bien/A menudo

c. ¿Dónde están vuestras maletas?   Siempre/Allí/Mañana

d. ¿Cómo prefiere viajar?   Recientemente/Ya/Tranquilamente

e. ¿Cuándo vamos para Suiza?   Pronto/Lentamente/Lejos

f. ¿Dónde está Toledo?   Lejos/Mal/Mucho

g. ¿Cuánto os costó el viaje?   Mucho/Mañana/A veces

h. ¿Cómo está tu amigo?   Mañana/Bien/Lentamente

i. ¿Te gusta volar?   Nunca/Rápidamente/Bastante

9. Translate into Spanish (easier).

a. I fly a lot.

____

b. I travel to London often.

____

c. We never go to Spain.

____

d. I have already bought a ticket.

____

e. Sometimes I walk to work.

____

f. Yesterday, I visited the market.

____

g. Recently, she went to Chile by plane.

____

10. Translate into Spanish (harder).

a. In the summer we often travel to Spain by car.

b. I will go to Scotland soon.

c. After visiting Buenos Aires, we went to Rosario by train.

d. Sometimes I prefer to arrive early at my destination.

e. Have you already visited Switzerland by train?

f. We really want to go to France next year.

g. I can travel directly to my destination by car.

h. Fortunately, the weather was good in Bolivia last year.

i. I never travel abroad by plane.

j. Do you regularly fly to London or take the car?

k. We always like to visit new countries.

l. I will book tickets online before going to Montreal.

m. We stay often in England, even if the weather is bad.

n. Next year I will probably not go on holiday.

Unit 4 - Preparing for speaking and writing

1. Split sentences.

El hotel era	nuevos países.
Estoy de	fui a Canadá.
Voy a	muy bonito pero caro.
Prefiero	vacaciones junto al mar.
El verano pasado	montar en bicicleta.
Normalmente	volar a viajar en tren.
Casi nunca voy al	vivir en otros países.
Me gusta descubrir	voy al aeropuerto en taxi.
Mi sueño es	extranjero.

2. Broken words.

a. Vac_ _ _ _ _ _ _   *Holidays*

b. Me_ _ _ _ de transporte   *Means of transport*

c. D_ _ _ubrir   *Discover*

d. En el ca_ _ _   *In the countryside*

e. Al_ _ _ _iento   *Accommodation*

f. Al_ _ _ _ar un co_ _ _   *To rent a car*

g. P_ _ar una se_ _ _ _   *To spend a week*

h. Per_ _ _ una mal_ _ _   *To lose a suitcase*

i. Pro_ _ _ la comida local   *To try local food*

j. A la or_ _ _ _ del m_ _   *By the seaside*

3. Complete the Spanish translation (all the verbs are in past simple):

a. El _________ pasado fui a ________.   *Last year I went to Colombia.*

b. _________ en avión y después _________ una bicicleta.   *I travelled by plane and then I rented a bike.*

c. Nosotros _________ un hotel enfrente del _________.   *We chose a hotel in front of the sea.*

d. Por la _________ fui a la _________.   *In the morning I went to the beach.*

e. _________ en el mar y _________ un libro.   *I swam in the sea and I read a book.*

f. Me ___________ dando largos paseos.   *I relaxed by going for long walks.*

g. Por la noche _________ y _________.   *At night I went out and danced.*

h. _________ la cocina _________, que estaba muy buena.   *I tried the local cuisine which was very good.*

i. Mi _________ es _________ a Estados Unidos.   *My dream is to go to the USA.*

4. Tangled translation: translate into Spanish.

a. *I went* de vacaciones

b. Viajar *abroad*

c. Viajar *by boat*

d. Nadar en *the river*

e. Un *accommodation* caro

f. *To choose* un apartamento

g. Unas *views* fantásticas

h. Los lugares *historic*

i. *To spend* una semana

j. Yo me *relaxed*

k. Yo *visited* un museo

5. Complete the answers to the questions.

a. ¿Adónde fuiste de vacaciones el año pasado?
b. F_ _ a Marruecos con mi f_ _ _ _ _ _.

a. ¿Cómo viajaste?
b. V_ _ _ _ en a_ _ _ _.

a. ¿Dónde te alojaste?
b. Me a_ _ _ _ en un hotel enfrente del m_ _.

a. ¿Cómo fue el viaje?
b. Fue m_ _ bien pero demasiado c_ _ _.

a. ¿Qué hiciste?
b. N_ _ _ en el mar y l_ _ un libro.

a. ¿Qué cosas interesantes viste?
b. Vi muchos animales y varios l_ _ _ _ _ _ históricos.

6. Complete each sentence with a suitable conjugated verb.

a. Yo _____________ en avión.

b. Yo _____________ unos billetes.

c. Yo _____________ varios lugares históricos.

d. Yo _____________ la comida local.

e. Yo _____________ cinco días en Japón.

f. Yo me ___________ en la playa.

g. Yo __________ un paseo por la orilla del mar.

h. Yo _____________ un coche por diez días.

i. Yo _____________ un tren a Barcelona.

j. Yo _____________ a mi destino a las diez.

7. Sentence puzzle: reorder the words.

a. de vacaciones fui Marruecos Yo a

____

b. caro Me en un alojé hotel

____

c. visitar Me lugares encanta históricos

____

d. Prefiero a montaña la ir

____

e. dos en semanas Pasé la República Dominicana

____

f. encanta Me ir países a extranjeros

____

8. Correct the mistakes in the bits underlined.

a. <u>Alojé</u> en un hotel tres estrellas.

b. <u>Yo he viajé</u> en bicicleta y en tren.

c. El año pasadó <u>voy a ir</u> a Panamá.

d. Normalmente voy <u>al escuela</u> en autobús.

e. <u>Yo saliste</u> con mis amigos todas las tardes.

f. <u>Relajé</u> escuchando música en la playa.

g. El <u>ano</u> que viene <u>fui</u> a Guatemala.

h. Nosotros probamos <u>el comida</u> local.

9. Add the missing accents.

a. Fui a la playa en autobus.

b. Me encanta visitar paises extranjeros.

c. Voy todos los dias a la escuela en coche.

d. Me aloje en un hotel cerca de la playa.

e. Descanse mucho tiempo en la playa.

f. Escuche musica en el coche.

g. Prefiero los lugares historicos.

h. He hablado frances durante las vacaciones.

10. Translate into Spanish.

a. I often like to take the train and the plane. _______________________________________

b. I prefer the train because it is fast and clean. _______________________________________

c. The plane is bad for the environment. _______________________________________

d. Yesterday, I went to the beach by car. _______________________________________

e. I usually go to school on foot. _______________________________________

f. Fortunately, we do not need a car. _______________________________________

g. Near my home there are shops and hotels. _______________________________________

h. There was an amazing view of the sea. _______________________________________

i. I discovered little streets and ate delicious food. _______________________________________

j. I hope to return to Peru next year. _______________________________________

Unit 4 - Writing and speaking from a photo card

Write something about both of these photos. Write about who you see, where they are and what they are doing. Read out your description.

Answer the following questions related to this topic. Read out your answers.

1. ¿Qué medio de transporte prefieres? ¿Por qué?

2. ¿Cómo vas a la escuela normalmente?

3. ¿Qué opinas sobre el transporte público en tu ciudad o región?

4. ¿Qué tipo de vacaciones prefieres? ¿Por qué?

5. ¿Qué hiciste el verano pasado durante las vacaciones?

Unit 4 - Speaking in a role-play

Look at the instructions on the left as they would appear in a speaking test. Read aloud with a partner the dialogue on the right. Then do the dialogue a second time, changing the answers or questions in bold. Take turns playing the two roles.

Foundation: at the hotel reception

<table>
<tr>
<td>

1. Describe a problem in your room.

2. Say where your room is.

3. Say how many nights you are staying.

4. Say what you think about the hotel.

5. Ask a question about restaurants near the hotel.

</td>
<td>

1. ¿Le puedo ayudar?
   Sí, por favor, tengo un problema con la televisión.

2. Lo siento. ¿Dónde está su habitación?
   En el segundo piso.

3. ¿Cuántas noches se va a quedar?
   Tres (noches).

4. ¿Qué le parece el hotel?
   Es un poco caro.

5. ¿Tiene alguna pregunta?
   ¿Hay algún restaurante italiano cerca del hotel?

</td>
</tr>
</table>

Higher: at the tourist office

<table>
<tr>
<td>

1. Say why you have come to the tourist office.

2. Say when you arrived in the town.

3. Describe something you have done already.

4. Ask a question about the town.

5. Say something you will do tomorrow.

</td>
<td>

1. Hola, ¿puedo ayudarle?
   Busco información sobre el festival de música.

2. ¿Cuándo llegó a la ciudad?
   (Llegué) el sábado pasado.

3. ¿Qué ha hecho hasta ahora?
   He visitado el castillo.

4. ¿Tiene alguna pregunta?
   ¿Hay algún cine en el centro de la ciudad?

5. ¿Qué va a hacer mañana?
   Mañana quiero ir a la piscina municipal.

</td>
</tr>
</table>

Unit 4 - Foundation writing

Write approximately 50 words in Spanish. Mention all points. Refer to the language in this unit, for example the Foundation Sentence Bank, or do the task in exam conditions, without help. Or do both!

- What means of transport you prefer   • What you think of trains   • What type of holidays you like
- What you are doing this summer   • What you think of camping

1. ____

2. ____

3. ____

4. ____

5. ____

Using your knowledge of grammar, complete the sentences below, choosing one of the three options given.

1   Este verano nos ____________ en Costa Rica (quedaremos/quedar/quedaré).

2   Mi madre ____________ el tren todos los días (tomaste/toma/tomaban).

3   El fin de semana pasado yo ____________ un castillo (visito/visitaré/visité).

4   Vimos un monumento muy ____________ (antiguos/antiguo/antigua).

5   A mi madre le encanta ____________ en avión (viajar/viaja/viajó).

Foundation/Higher writing

Write approximately 90 words in Spanish. You must refer to each bullet point.

- Holidays you like.   • What you did last summer on holiday.   • Where you would like to travel in the future.

____

____

____

____

____

____

____

Higher writing

Write approximately 150 words about travel in Spanish. Cover both bullet points. Refer to the language in this unit, for example the Higher Sentence Bank, or do the task in exam conditions, without help. Or do both!

- The advantages and disadvantages of travelling by plane.
- A long journey you made somewhere in the past.

Foundation sentence bank

Me gusta tomar el tren y el avión.	I like to take the train and the plane.
Prefiero el tren porque es rápido y limpio.	I prefer the train because it is fast and clean.
El avión es malo para el medio ambiente.	The plane is bad for the environment.
Fui a la playa en coche.	I went to the beach by car.
Yo voy al colegio a pie.	I go to school on foot.
No necesitamos coche.	We do not need a car.
Cerca de la playa hay tiendas y hoteles.	Near the beach there are shops and hotels.
El turismo es malo para el medio ambiente.	Tourism is bad for the environment.
El año pasado fui a Francia.	Last year I went to France.
El verano que viene voy a Inglaterra.	Next summer I am going to England.
Me gustan las vacaciones junto al mar.	I like holidays by the sea.
Durante las vacaciones compré algunos recuerdos.	During the holidays I bought some souvenirs.
Me gusta el campo porque es tranquilo.	I like the countryside because it is quiet.
Prefiero las vacaciones en el extranjero.	I prefer holidays abroad.

Higher sentence bank

El tren siempre está más limpio que el avión.	The train is always cleaner than the plane.
Me encanta viajar en tren porque es muy rápido.	I love travelling by train because it's very fast.
La bicicleta es mejor para la salud.	Cycling is better for your health.
A pesar de la contaminación, el coche es muy práctico.	Despite the pollution, the car is very practical.
El transporte público es rápido y puntual.	Public transport is fast and on time.
Hablé mucho durante mi visita a Francia.	I spoke a lot during my visit to France.
Allí se puede dar paseos por las montañas.	There, you can do walks in the mountains.
Tengo la intención de quedarme en Inglaterra este año.	I intend to stay in England this year.
Había una buena vista del mar.	There was a good view of the sea.
Descubrí pequeñas calles y restaurantes.	I discovered little streets and restaurants.
Espero volver a España el año que viene.	I hope to return to Spain next year.
Lo que más me gusta es cuando hace buen tiempo.	What I like most is when the weather is good.
Me gustaría visitar Australia algún día.	I would like to visit Australia one day.
Nunca olvidaré esas vacaciones.	I will never forget those holidays.

UNIT 5

Free time activities

Contents

- Foundation vocab building
- Foundation reading
- Higher vocab building
- Higher reading
- Grammar focus: Imperfect Tense
- Preparing for speaking and writing
- Writing and speaking from a photo card
- Speaking in a role play
- Writing
- Sentence banks

Unit 5 - Foundation vocab building

Vocabulary

a menudo	*often*
a veces	*sometimes*
activo	*active*
el/la amigo/a	*friend*
aprender	*to learn*
el/la autor/a	*author*
bailar	*to dance*
la bicicleta (bici)	*bicycle*
cantar	*to sing*
el cine	*cinema*
charlar	*to chat*
chatear	*to chat (online)*
las compras	*shopping*
el concierto	*concert*
correr	*to run*
demasiado	*too much/many*
descargar	*to download*
la televisión	*television*
emocionante	*exciting*
en línea	*online*
el equipo	*team*
escribir	*to write*
escuchar	*to listen*
el estadio	*stadium*
hacer	*to do/make*
el grupo	*group, band*
el instrumento	*instrument*
intentar	*to try*
el interés	*interest*
interesarse	*to be interested*
la lectura	*reading*
leer	*to read*
el libro	*book*
el miembro	*member*
el móvil	*mobile phone*
la música	*music*
la natación	*swimming*
la novela	*novel*
la pantalla	*screen*
participar	*to take part (in)*
el partido	*match*
pasar	*to spend (time)*
el paseo	*walk*
perder	*to lose*
el portátil	*laptop*
salir	*to go out*
siempre	*always*
también	*also*
el teatro	*theatre*
ver	*to see/watch*
el videojuego	*videogame*

1. Match up.

Nadar	To dance
Jugar	To play
Leer	To lose
Correr	To listen
Aprender	To swim
Descargar	To read
Perder	To do
Hacer	To watch
Ver	To learn
Escuchar	To run
Bailar	To download

2. Correct the wrong translations.

a. Me encanta cantar: *I love to run.*

b. Me gustaría leer: *I would like to swim.*

c. Me gustaba correr: *I used to like to write.*

d. Me gusta jugar: *I like to do.*

e. Odio aprender: *I hate to take.*

f. Pierdo a menudo: *I often lose.*

g. Bailé un poco: *I danced a bit.*

h. Nado a menudo: *I often go out.*

3. One of three: circle the right answer.

Ver	*To veer*	*To eat*	*To watch*
Escribir	*To read*	*To write*	*To draw*
Bicicleta	*Bike*	*Scooter*	*Car*
Emocionante	*Exciting*	*Amazing*	*Emotional*
A veces	*Often*	*Never*	*Sometimes*
Portátil	*Mobile*	*Table*	*Laptop*
Novela	*Poem*	*Paper*	*Novel*
Perder	*To win*	*To lose*	*To play*
Estadio	*Stadium*	*State*	*Step*
Ganar	*To win*	*To lose*	*To play*

4. Tick words that refer to technology.

a. Portátil

b. Natación

c. Descargar

d. Ordenador

e. Estadio

f. En línea

g. Paseo

h. Pantalla

5. Complete the translation.

a. Veo un programa: *I watch a ________________.*

b. Monto en bicicleta: *I ride a ________________.*

c. Descargo música: *I ________________ music.*

d. Estoy leyendo una novela: *I'm reading a ________________.*

e. Paso una hora chateando: *I spend an hour __________ _________.*

f. Salgo con mi novio: *I ________ _______ with my boyfriend.*

6. Translate into English.

Español	Inglés	Español	Inglés
Siempre		Perder	
A menudo		Pasar	
A veces		Descargar	
Nunca		Interesarse	

7. Sentence puzzle: put the words in each sentence in the right order.

a. en Juego todos móvil mi los días   *I play on my mobile phone every day.*

____

b. No mucho deporte hago   *I don't do a lot of sport.*

____

c. dos Yo paso día en horas al internet   *I spend two hours per day on the internet.*

____

d. Me dar gusta en el paseo un parque   *I like to go for a walk in the park.*

____

e. salgo A con menudo después del mi novio colegio   *I often go out with my boyfriend after school.*

____

f. pasatiempo Mi favorito en bicicleta es montar   *My favourite hobby is to go cycling.*

____

g. películas de y programas Veo música   *I watch films and music programmes.*

____

8. Complete with the correct option.

a. Yo ___________ una película de horror.

b. Yo ___________ en bicicleta.

c. Yo ___________ a videojuegos.

d. Yo ___________ una hora en TikTok.

e. Yo ___________ en el teléfono.

f. Yo ___________ con mi novia.

g. Yo ___________ a un centro comercial.

h. Yo ___________ una novela.

> montaré
> hablé
> iré
> juego
> leo
> salí
> paso
> veo

9. Translate into English.

a. Fui al estadio.

____

b. Paso una hora en YouTube.

____

c. Hice deporte.

____

d. Veré un programa de televisión.

____

e. Antes, siempre escuchaba K-Pop.

____

f. Saldría con mis amigos.

____

10. Tick all the words with negative meaning.

a. Bonito.

b. Simpático.

c. Aburrido.

d. Horrible.

e. Gracioso.

f. Incorrecto.

g. Peligroso.

h. Perder.

i. Pésimo.

j. Malo.

k. Bien.

11. Translate into English.

a. Me gusta el fútbol y la música. Mi estilo preferido es el hip hop.

b. Me encanta leer. Mis novelas favoritas son las policíacas.

c. Toco la guitarra y el piano. Además, me gusta dibujar.

d. No toco ningún instrumento pero me gustaría aprender.

e. Cuando hace buen tiempo monto en bicicleta en el campo.

f. Me gustaría ir de compras con mis amigos.

g. Me encanta jugar a videojuegos con amigos.

h. Ayer por la tarde vi una serie de televisión. Era genial.

i. Me gusta salir de fiesta con mis amigos. ¡Me encanta bailar!

j. ¡El fin de semana pasado jugué con mi ordenador durante 10 horas!

k. El fin de semana que viene iré a casa de mi amiga Martina.

Unit 5 - Foundation reading

1.   Read these comments from young people about their free time activities.

Antonio
Me encanta leer; ¡siempre tengo una novela pendiente! Además, el fin de semana me gusta salir con mis amigas. A veces vamos al cine.

Víctor
Mi pasatiempo favorito es el ciclismo. Salgo todos los domingos con amigos. También me gusta jugar con el ordenador.

Carla
No tengo muchas aficiones, pero me gusta hablar con mis amigos y los sábados por la mañana juego en un equipo de fútbol.

Who says what? Put a cross in the correct column for each question.

Who says this?	Antonio	Víctor	Carla
a. They play for a team on Saturdays.			
b. They love reading.			
c. They go cycling.			
d. They do not have many pastimes.			
e. They play computer games.			
f. They go out to watch a film.			

2.   Read what Frank says about how he spends his free time.

Me gusta ver partidos de fútbol en el estadio. Esta temporada mi equipo no está jugando bien, pero me gusta pasar tiempo con mi amigo Pablo y ver los partidos juntos.

Además, los fines de semana ayudo a mi abuela, que trabaja en su jardín. A veces voy a la ciudad con mi hermano o salgo con mis amigos. Los sábados por la mañana también trabajo en una cafetería. Vendo helados.

Complete the gap in each sentence using a word from the box below. There are more words than gaps.

---

well	kitchen	coffee
ice-creams	badly	garden

---

a.   This season, Frank's team is playing ________________.

b.   He helps his grandmother in the ________________.

c.   On Saturday mornings he sells ________________.

Unit 5 - Foundation reading

3.   Read what these people say about computer gaming.

Amanda
Los videojuegos son una parte muy importante en mi vida. Todos los días juego alrededor de dos horas.

Mohamed
A veces juego a videojuegos y me gusta. Sin embargo, creo que jugar muchas horas es una pérdida de tiempo.

Gustavo
Creo que la gente pasa demasiado tiempo con el ordenador. Tenemos que salir más y hacer algo de deporte.

Helena
En mi opinión, los videojuegos son malos para la salud. Estar horas y horas delante de una pantalla no es bueno.

If the person has a positive opinion put P in the box. If they have a negative opinion put N in the box. If they express both a positive and negative opinion put P/N in the box.

Amanda ⬚   Mohamed ⬚   Gustavo ⬚   Helena ⬚

4.   Sandra is talking about her favourite sport.

Mi deporte favorito es la natación. Voy a la piscina con un amigo los domingos por la mañana para nadar una hora. La natación es un deporte muy sano.

Empecé a nadar cuando era muy pequeña. Aprendí con mi tía. También es un deporte muy útil. Por ejemplo, si estás en el mar, es menos peligroso si sabes nadar.

Tick the best answer in each case, then answer the last question in English.

1. Sandra's favourite sport is: a) horse-riding   b) running   c) swimming

2. She does this on: a) Sunday mornings   b) Saturday   c) Sunday afternoons

3. She says the sport is: a) tiring   b) healthy   c) expensive

4. She began the sport: a) a year ago   b) very young   c) recently

5. She learned with: a) her mother   b) her uncle   c) her aunt

6. What does she say about the usefulness of the sport? Mention two details.

____

Unit 5 - Foundation reading

5. Read about football in Equatorial Guinea, Africa.

El fútbol es una de las grandes pasiones de los jóvenes de Guinea Ecuatorial. Se juega en todas partes. Los niños empiezan a jugar a una edad muy temprana. Para muchos adolescentes de Guinea, el fútbol no es sólo un pasatiempo, es una forma de vida.

Une a la gente y muchos jóvenes quieren jugar en un equipo grande. Las chicas también juegan al fútbol, pero a menudo menos que los chicos.

a. Where do young people play? _______________________________________

b. How is football described in Guinea Equatorial (for teenagers)? ____________________________

c. What do many young people want? _______________________________________

d. What is said about girls' football? Mention two points.

____

6. Read what Adrián says about his favourite pastime.

Paso mucho tiempo escribiendo canciones. Es bastante difícil, así que a veces recurro a la IA* para que me ayude. Mis canciones son bastante originales. Por ejemplo, el fin de semana pasado escribí una canción sobre un personaje de una novela. En el futuro, en vez de escribir, me gustaría tocar en un grupo.

* IA = AI (Artificial Intelligence)

a. What does Adrián do? _______________________________________

b. Why does he use AI? _______________________________________

c. What did he do last weekend? _______________________________________

d. What would he like to do in the future? _______________________________________

7. Read what Jennifer says about sport.

Me encanta el deporte. De momento, hago deporte por mi cuenta. Hace poco empecé a montar en bicicleta, que me gusta mucho. Además, el año pasado jugué al fútbol en un equipo de chicas. Pero en mi nuevo colegio no hay equipo femenino. También me gustaba la natación, pero no tenía tiempo suficiente para practicarla. Quiero practicar otro deporte de equipo y, en la universidad, voy a empezar a correr.

What does Jennifer say about these sports? Write P for a sport she did in the past. N for a sport she does now, F for a sport she wants to do in the future.

a. Football [ ]   b. Swimming [ ]   c. Cycling [ ]   d. Running [ ]

Unit 5 - Higher vocabulary building

Vocabulary

a menudo	often
activo	active
el/la amigo/a	friend
aprender	to learn
el/la autor/a	author
bailar	to dance
la bicicleta (bici)	bicycle
cantar	to sing
el cine	cinema
la videoconsola	games console
charlar	to chat
chatear	to chat (online)
el concierto	concert
correr	to run
dar un paseo	go for a walk
demasiado	too much/too many
descansar	to rest
descargar	to download
emocionante	exciting
en línea	online
el equipo	team
escribir	to write
el estadio	stadium
fuera	outside
ganar	to win
hacer	to do
el instrumento	instrument
intentar	to try
el interés	interest
interesarse	to be interested
ir de compras	go shopping
el videojuego	videogame
la lectura	reading
leer	to read
el libro	book
el miembro	member
minusválido	disabled
la música	music
la natación	swimming
la novela	novel
la pantalla	screen
participar	to take part (in)
el partido	match
pasar	to spend (time)
el paseo	walk
perder	to lose
pertenecer a	to belong to
la pista/la cancha	ground, pitch
salir	to go out
la serie	series
la receta	recipe
relajarse	to relax
el teatro	theatre
la televisión (la tele)	television
ver	to see/watch

1. Match up.

Pantalla	Song
Ordenador	Novel
Libro	Online
Móvil	Game
Videojuego	Shopping
Juego	Reading
Lectura	Mobile phone
En línea	Videogame
Novela	Interest
Compras	Book
Interés	Computer
Canción	Screen

2. Correct the wrong translations.

a. Pasar	*To spend*
b. Aprender	*To steal*
c. Ganar	*To learn*
d. Perder	*To lose*
e. Leer	*To write*
f. Escribir	*To read*
g. Salir	*To download*
h. Descargar	*To run*

3. One of three: circle the right answers.

El gusto	*Taste*	*Game*	*Gust*
El equipo	*Team*	*Match*	*Pitch*
Correr	*To shop*	*To run*	*To walk*
Probar	*To try*	*To mix*	*To say*
El juego	*Jug*	*Match*	*Game*
La novela	*Novel*	*Novelty*	*Book*
Perder	*To win*	*To lose*	*To run*
La cancha	*Catcher*	*Pitch*	*Team*
Leer	*To read*	*To go*	*To run*
Pasar	*To run*	*To try*	*To spend*

4. Tick any verbs referring to physical activity.

a. Escuchar

b. Pasear

c. Leer

d. Nadar

e. Correr

f. Ver

g. Descansar

h. Bailar

i. Montar en bici

5. Complete the translations.

a. Yo vi una serie: *I watched a _____________.*

b. No hice nada: *I did ____________.*

c. Después de la escuela descansé: *After school I ____________.*

d. Me encanta leer novelas: *I love reading ___________.*

e. Aquí hay un campo de fútbol: *Here, there is a _________ _____.*

f. Yo hago natación a menudo: *I go ___________ often.*

g. A veces voy al teatro: *___________ I go to the theatre.*

h. Paso dos horas en Instagram: *I _______ two hours on Instagram.*

i. Me gustan los juegos de cartas: *I like card ___________.*

j. Me gusta escuchar música en mi móvil: *I like listening to music on my ___________ _____________.*

6. Match the opposites.

Perder	Genial
Siempre	Malsano
Aburrido	Ganar
Descansar	Barato
Horrible	Nunca
Sano	Poco
Demasiado	Cansarse
Salir	Divertido
Caro	Quedarse

7. Circle the correct option.

a. Hago varias *libros/compras/novelas.*

b. *Veo/tomo/paso* una serie.

c. *Perdí/leí/escribí* el partido.

d. Me *gusta/adoran/interesan* los idiomas.

e. *Veía/leía/escuchaba* la canción.

f. *Corro/tomo/paso* dos horas en línea.

g. *Intento/tomo/hago* aprender.

h. *Voy/hago/descanso* en bici.

i. Me gusta *hacer/leer/pasar* novelas.

8. Missing letters.

a. Pe_d_ r — *To lose*

b. No_e_ _ — *A novel*

c. _or_er — *To run*

d. Pa_ _ r — *To spend*

e. D_ sc_nsar — *To rest*

f. Ga_ _ r — *To earn*

g. C_m_ _ — *Pitch*

h. _a_ o — *Expensive*

i. In_en_ar — *To try*

9. Unjumble the words and translate.

e.g. irlbo: libro — book

a. erderp: ___________ ___________

b. agnra: ___________ ___________

c. inertsé: ___________ ___________

d. sliar: ___________ ___________

e. ntietanr: ___________ ___________

f. eler: ___________ ___________

g. sguto: ___________ ___________

10. Break the flow. Insert lines where there should be gaps.

a. Enmiopiniónesimportanteteneraficionesenlavida.

b. Nadoenlapiscinadesdehacecincoaños.

c. Meencantairalaplayacuandohacecalor.

d. Cuandoerapequeñabailabadosvecesalasemana.

e. Hedecididodarunpaseoenelcampo.

f. Elsábadopasadofuidecomprasconmisamigos.

g. Antesjugabaavideojuegosperoyanomeinteresan.

11. Complete with the correct verb from the grid at the bottom.

a. Antes ___________ novelas.

b. Ayer ___________ a jugar al tenis.

c. Mañana ___________ al centro comercial.

d. Me ___________ nadar.

e. ___________ una canción de hip hop.

f. ___________ de compras todos los sábados.

g. Me ___________ los videojuegos de fantasía.

h. Me ___________ en clase de yoga.

i. ___________ horas viendo vídeos en TikTok.

j. Esta noche voy a ___________ con mis amigos.

k. Me lo he ___________ bien.

l. ___________ la tele a menudo.

quedar	veo	escuché	leía
pasado	relajo	iré	aprendí
gustaría	paso	encantan	voy

12. Translate into English.

a. Es importante tener pasatiempos en la vida.

b. Hago natación desde hace cinco años.

c. Me encanta ir a la playa cuando hace buen tiempo.

d. Cuando era pequeña, solía bailar.

e. El domingo que viene vamos a ir al cine.

f. Después de comer, fui al teatro.

g. He decidido dar un paseo por el campo.

h. El sábado pasado fui de compras.

i. Antes jugaba a videojuegos…

j. …pero ya no me interesan.

k. Espero poder tocar un instrumento en el futuro.

l. Antes de ir a la piscina, vi a mis amigos en la ciudad.

m. Lo que más me gusta son las series de televisión.

n. Cuando era más joven hacía más deporte.

o. Reconozco que prefiero la música a la lectura.

p. Paso una o dos horas al día en YouTube.

Unit 5 - Higher reading

1. Read what Susana says about her free time. Then circle the best answer to complete each sentence.

Me encanta leer, sobre todo novelas, porque me permite vivir en mundos diferentes. A veces también veo series de televisión, sobre todo las que tienen historias originales. Otro pasatiempo mío es pasar tiempo al aire libre: me gusta montar en bicicleta, dar un paseo por la naturaleza o simplemente disfrutar del sol. Los videojuegos son también una de mis pasiones, sobre todo los últimos lanzamientos. Por último, antes no cocinaba mucho, pero ahora disfruto haciendo nuevas recetas.

Por el contrario, no me interesan ni la música ni la jardinería y no me gustan mucho ni el deporte ni ir de compras.

1. Susana likes: a. reading   b. music   c. travel

2. She also enjoys: a. history   b. TV series   c. gardening

3. What does she do outside? Mention three details. ___________________________

4. What video games does she prefer to play? ___________________________

5. She also enjoys: a. cooking   b. sport   c. shopping

2. Read Amina's message to a friend.

Las aficiones son importantes para mí porque necesito descansar después del trabajo. De hecho, hace poco empecé a cantar en la iglesia con varios amigos.

Con respecto al deporte, antes corría mucho pero ya no debido a un problema de espalda. Sin embargo, hoy en día hago un poco de ciclismo.

Si tengo tiempo, quizá empiece a tocar un instrumento musical.

Write P for something that happened in the past, N for something that is happening now, F for something that will happen in the future. Write the correct letter in each box.

a. Playing an instrument ☐   c. Singing ☐

b. Running ☐   d. Cycling ☐

3. Read this article about Carla, a musician in Panama. Then answer the questions in English.

Desde pequeña, Carla siempre ha soñado con actuar en público. Sus padres conocían su pasión por la música pero siempre pensaron que los estudios eran más importantes. Por eso, Carla terminó la universidad antes de embarcarse en su carrera musical. El sábado pasado, Carla cantó en una boda ante un centenar de personas. El año que viene publicará canciones en internet.

a. What was Carla's ambition? ___________________________

b. What did her parents think? ___________________________

c. What did she do before starting her career? ___________________________

d. What did she do last Saturday? ___________________________

e. What will happen next year? ___________________________

Unit 5 - Higher reading

4. Read this article about some of the most popular pastimes in Uruguay.

El deporte

Muchos uruguayos practican deporte para estar más fuertes, pesar menos o mantenerse sanos, entre otras razones. La oferta deportiva es muy amplia y se adapta a todas las necesidades, incluidas las de las personas con discapacidades. Desde correr hasta nadar, pasando por montar en bicicleta o bailar, ¡hay un deporte para cada uno!

Actividades culturales

Los uruguayos también aprecian la cultura. Los eventos culturales son una buena manera de relajarse y conocer gente nueva. Por eso, las visitas al teatro, los conciertos y los museos son muy populares. Hay que decir que la música encabeza la lista, muy por delante del cine. La mayoría de los uruguayos escucha música todos los días.

Videojuegos

Los ordenadores y las videoconsolas desempeñan un papel importante en el mundo de los pasatiempos de los uruguayos. Según un estudio del Ministerio de Industria, Energía y Minería, el número de descargas de *videojuegos nacionales superó los 10 millones.

*videojuegos creados en Uruguay

---

   a. Why do people do sport? Mention three details.   _______________________________

       ____

   b. Mention three sports referred to.   _______________________________

   c. Give two reasons why people do cultural activities.   _______________________________

   d. What is said about music? Mention two details.   _______________________________

   e. What exactly does the Ministry of Industry, Energy and Mining say? _______________________________

       ____

5. Read about what Irene wrote in her diary about last weekend.

El sábado por la mañana fui de compras con mis amigas. Pasamos mucho tiempo probándonos ropa y divirtiéndonos juntas. Por la tarde, fuimos a un parque donde había un pequeño concierto de música. Nos pareció un poco aburrido, pero fue estupendo disfrutar del buen tiempo primaveral.

El domingo por la tarde vi una película en casa con mi familia. Fue estupendo pasar tiempo juntos. Por la noche, leí una nueva novela antes de acostarme.

   a. What did she and her friends do on Saturday morning? _______________________________

   b. What did they do exactly? Mention two details.   _______________________________

   c. After that, what did they think of the music concert?   _______________________________

   d. What did she do on Sunday afternoon?   _______________________________

   e. What did she do before bed?   _______________________________

Unit 5 - Higher reading

6. Read these diary extracts from Josué, a boy from Honduras, a country in Central America.

Lunes 26 de marzo
Hoy he ayudado a mi padre a reparar su moto. Ha sido difícil, pero he aprendido mucho con él. Luego he jugado al fútbol en el parque con mi equipo. Aunque hemos perdido ha sido una buena oportunidad para relajarnos y divertirnos juntos.

Miércoles 28 de marzo
Esta tarde he decidido ir a la biblioteca a estudiar. He encontrado un libro sobre la historia de Honduras que me ha parecido muy interesante. Me he quedado allí durante horas. Mis amigos creen que estoy loco.

Viernes 30 de marzo
Para terminar la semana, he cocinado un poco con mi madre. Hemos hecho una receta que no habíamos hecho nunca. A lo mejor algún día abro un restaurante.

a. What did he do with his father on 26th March? _______________________________

b. What did he like about the football game? Mention two details.

____

c. What did he do on Wednesday afternoon? Mention two details.

____

d. What do his friends think about him? _______________________________

e. What does he say about the recipe he made? _______________________________

f. What does he say at the end? _______________________________

7. Read about Silvia's plans for this weekend. Then tick the best options.

Ayer pensaba que iba a ir a la playa o a montar en bicicleta, pero en realidad hoy, sábado, voy a la ciudad con mis amigas. Quiero encontrar el vestido perfecto para una fiesta en casa de mis primos. Luego, por la tarde, en vez de ir al cine, vamos a dar un paseo. Quería ir a casa de mi mejor amiga, pero está enferma.

El domingo, después de hacer los deberes, voy a ir a casa de mis abuelos a comer en su jardín y después daré una vuelta en bici por el bosque. Al final del día, iré a una clase de baile.

1. On Saturday morning she is… a. going to the beach   b. riding her bike   c. going shopping

2. On Saturday afternoon she will… a. visit her best friend   b. see a film   c. go for a walk

3. On Sunday, after lunch, she will… a. go for a bike ride   b. do her homework   c. have a dance lesson

Unit 5 - Grammar focus: Imperfect Tense

Uses of the imperfect tense

Forming this tense is easy, but knowing when to use it can be more challenging. We are going to learn three uses of the imperfect tense:

1. Actions that were repeated in the past

- De pequeña **jugaba** al fútbol todos los días.   *As a child, I **used to play** football every day.*
- Antes mi madre **iba** a Madrid cada año.   *Before, my mother **used to go** to Madrid every year.*

In these cases the verb describes actions repeated in the past, both often (first sentence) or only from time to time (second sentence). If your sentence contains "I used to…", it is very likely to require the imperfect in Spanish.

2. An action that interrupts another action (or occurs simultaneously) in the past

- **Estaba yendo** al pueblo cuando vi a mi amiga.   *I **was going** into town when I saw my friend.*
- Yo **trabajaba** mientras mi padre **cocinaba**.   *I **was working** while my dad **was cooking**.*

In these cases the imperfect is used to describe actions that encompass other actions that occur simultaneously. Think of "while" or "at the same time as": while I was going into town, I saw my friend.

3. Description in the past

Lastly, the imperfect is used to describe people, places, situations, etc. in the past. Look at these:

- Mi casa **era** grande y bonita.   *My house **was** big and beautiful.*
- Valeria **tenía** el pelo rizado y largo.   *Valerie **had** long and curly hair.*

The most commonly used descriptive verbs are:

Estar	*To be*	**Estaba** muy nervioso/a antes del examen. *I was very nervous before the exam.*
Ser	*To be*	Cuando **era** pequeño/a **era** muy activo/a. *When I was little I used to be very active.*
Hacer + calor/frío/buen/mal tiempo *The weather is hot/cold/good/bad*		**Hacía** buen tiempo así que fuimos al cine. *The weather was good so we went to the cinema.*
Haber	*There is/are*	**Había** un problema en mi habitación (en el hotel). *There was a problem in my room (in the hotel).*
Llevar (ropa)	*To wear*	**Llevaba** un abrigo rojo porque hacía frío. *I/he/she was wearing a red coat because it was cold.*
Parecer	*To look like/appear*	El vestido **parecía** caro, pero no lo **era**. *The dress appeared expensive, but it was not.*
Tener	*To have*	**Tenía** una mascota cuando era pequeño/a. *I had a pet when I was little.*

Recognising the imperfect tense

For each sentence, decide if the sentence is in the Present (PRES), Perfect (PERF) or Imperfect Tense (IMP), as in the example.

e.g. *Solía jugar al fútbol con mis amigas.*	**IMP**
Me gusta ir al cine los fines de semana.	
Ahora tengo muchas aficiones.	
He ido a nadar con dos amigas mías.	
Yo paseaba a menudo por la ciudad con mi novio.	
Había una piscina no muy lejos de la estación de tren.	
Hay un polideportivo cerca de mi casa.	
He visto a mi amiga Celia en la cafetería.	
Siempre veo a mis amigos en el centro comercial.	
Hago danza y yoga.	
Hacía más deporte cuando era más joven.	
He salido a pasear por la playa con mi novia.	
Normalmente monto en bici cuando hace buen tiempo.	
Me gustaba ir en bici por el campo.	

Conjugating the imperfect

To conjugate regular verbs in imperfect, you only need to learn two different sets of conjugation endings for the regular verbs: one set for the verbs ending -AR (-aba), and a second set for the verbs ending in -ER and -IR (-ía).

As in most verb tenses, to conjugate verbs in the imperfect, you need to remove the ending -AR, -ER or -IR from the infinitive form and add the conjugation ending to the verb stem.

<table>
<tr><td colspan="3" align="center">Imperfect tense - regular verbs: -AR, -ER & -IR</td></tr>
<tr><td align="center">HABLAR
(to talk)</td><td align="center">COMER
(to eat)</td><td align="center">VIVIR
(to live)</td></tr>
<tr><td align="center">Yo hablaba
(I used to talk)</td><td align="center">Yo comía</td><td align="center">Yo vivía</td></tr>
<tr><td align="center">Tú hablabas
(you sing. used to talk)</td><td align="center">Tú comías</td><td align="center">Tú vivías</td></tr>
<tr><td align="center">Él/ella/usted hablaba
(he/she/you sing. formal used to talk)</td><td align="center">Él/ella/usted comía</td><td align="center">Él/ella/usted vivías</td></tr>
<tr><td align="center">Nosotros/as hablábamos
(we used to talk)</td><td align="center">Nosotros/as comíamos</td><td align="center">Nosotros/as vivíamos</td></tr>
<tr><td align="center">Vosotros/as hablabais
(you pl. used to talk)</td><td align="center">Vosotros/as comíais</td><td align="center">Vosotros/as vivíais</td></tr>
<tr><td align="center">Ellos/as/ustedes hablaban
(they/you pl. formal used to talk)</td><td align="center">Ellos/as/ustedes comían</td><td align="center">Ellos/as/ustedes vivían</td></tr>
</table>

Imperfect tense - irregular verbs

IR (to go)	SER (to be)	VER (to see)
Yo **iba** (I used to go)	Yo **era**	Yo **veía**
Tú **ibas** (You sing. used to go)	Tú **eras**	Tú **veías**
Él/ella/usted **iba** (He/she/you sing. formal used to go)	Él/ella/usted **era**	Él/ella/usted **veía**
Nosotros/as **íbamos** (We used to go)	Nosotros/as **éramos**	Nosotros/as **veíamos**
Vosotros/as **ibais** (You pl. used to go)	Vosotros/as **erais**	Vosotros/as **veíais**
Ellos/ellas/ustedes **iban** (They/you pl. formal used to go)	Ellos/as/ustedes **eran**	Ellos/as/ustedes **veían**

1. Match up (the solutions for "Yo" and "Marc" are interchangeable).

Nosotras	nadabas en la piscina.
Tú	jugaba al fútbol.
Yo	veíamos el partido.
Marc	jugabais al ajedrez.
Vosotros	bailaban.
Ellas	iba en bicicleta.

2. Circle the best verb in each sentence.

a. Yo *caminaba/hacía/me gustaba* a la escuela todos los días.

b. A ustedes les *hacían/eran/gustaba* ir al cine muy a menudo.

c. Mi hermana *hacía/venía/compraba* a la piscina conmigo.

d. En verano *era/hacía/tenía* buen tiempo todos los días.

e. Ellas *corrían/tenían/hacían* cuando tuve un accidente.

f. Me *iba/encantaba/escribía* ir a clases de baile los jueves.

g. ¿Tú *comías/bebías/fumabas* muchos dulces de pequeño?

3. Present to imperfect.

a. Yo voy al cine.   Yo **iba** al cine.

b. Yo juego al fútbol.   _______________

c. Yo monto en bici.   _______________

d. Yo salgo con mis amigos.   _______________

e. Yo soy muy deportista.   _______________

f. Yo tengo muchos amigos.   _______________

g. Me gusta la música.   _______________

h. Me encanta leer.   _______________

4. Complete the sentence with the best verb in imperfect.

a. Yo j________ a menudo al fútbol.

b. Mi hermano b_______ en la discoteca.

c. Nosotros p__________ mucho tiempo en el campo.

d. Vosotros l_______ muchos libros.

e. Yo e_______ cuentos.

f. ¿Tú e______________ música a menudo?

g. Usted i_______ al parque casi todos los días.

h. Yo e_______ feliz cuando yo _______ pequeño.

5. Answer creatively as if you were your child self!

a. ¿Ibas al parque?   No, iba a la piscina.

b. ¿Veías películas de horror? _______________________

c. ¿Eras activo/a?   _______________________

d. ¿Tenías muchos amigos? _______________________

e. ¿Salías a menudo?   _______________________

f. ¿Te gustaba leer?   _______________________

g. ¿Tenías muchos deberes? _______________________

h. ¿Jugabas a videojuegos? _______________________

i. ¿Bebías cerveza?   _______________________

6. Insert the missing vowels.

a. Y_ c_m_ _ d_lc_s.

b. N_s_tr_s j_g_b_m_s _ l_s c_rt_s.

c. _ll_s d_b_n m_ch_s p_s_ _s.

d. _ll_ _b_ _ l_ d_sc_t_c_.

e. ¿_b_ _s _l _st_d_ _ d_ p_q_ _ñ_s?

f. Y_ v_ _ _ s_r_ _s d_ t_l_v_s_ _n.

g. _st_d l_ _ _ n_v_l_s.

h. T_ j_g_b_s _n _l p_rq_ _.

i. Y_ _r_ m_s d_p_rt_st_.

7. Choose the right verb from the grid.

a. Yo _______ mucho durante mi tiempo libre.

b. Tú ______ muchos pasatiempos cuando tenías 9 años.

c. Yo antes _______ al fútbol pero ya no lo hago.

d. Nosotros _______ a menudo al campo.

e. Vosotros _______ de compras a la ciudad los sábados.

f. Cuando yo ______ más joven, leía más libros.

g. Mi madre _______ más activa cuando era más joven.

h. Me ___________ jugar a videojuegos.

ibais	leía	era	íbamos
jugaba	era	encantaba	tenías

8. Translate into Spanish using the imperfect.

a. I used to play football with my friends.

____

b. I used to be more sporty than now.

____

c. We used to go to the cinema a lot.

____

d. What were you doing yesterday?

____

e. I was talking to my friends in class.

____

9. What did you do on weekdays as a child? Use the times & activities to write Spanish sentences.

a. A las ocho de la mañana, yo ___________________________

b. A las diez, yo_______________________________

c. _______________________________

d. _______________________________

e. _______________________________

f. _______________________________

g. _______________________________

h. _______________________________

i. _______________________________

j. _______________________________

k. _______________________________

l. _______________________________

a. 8:00	Going to school
b. 10:00	Working in class
c. 11:00	Talking with friends
d. 12:00	Speaking Spanish
e. 12:30	Eating at school
f. 15:30	Returning home
g. 18:00	Doing homework
h. 19:00	Messaging a friend
i. 20:00	Watching a series
j. 21:00	Listening to music
k. 21:30	Drinking some milk
l. 22:00	Going to bed

Unit 5 - Preparing for speaking and writing

1. Missing letter challenge.

a. L_eré una nove_a.   *I will read a novel.*
b. J_ gu_ con mi m_vil.   *I played on my phone.*
c. _eo una _erie.   *I watch a series.*
d. Me rel_ _o en mi hab_tación. *I relax in my room.*
e. Sal_o con mi a_ _go.   *I go out with my friend.*
f. Jug_b_ al f_tbol.   *I used to play football.*
g. Es_uchar_ música.   *I will listen to music.*
h. Ir_a al cent_o co_ercial. *I would go to the mall.*
i. C_ _rí en el parque.   *I ran in the park.*
j. C_ateo con mi_ ami_os.   *I chat with my friends.*

2. Complete with *iba, hacía, era* o *jugaba* as appropriate.

a. Antes, _______ al cine con mi novia.
b. De pequeño no _______ nada.
c. De niño _______ al centro comercial.
d. Hace unos años _______ en bicicleta.
e. En 2003, _______ con mi ordenador.
f. De joven _______ muy deportista.
g. Antes, _______ más deporte.
h. Hace tres años _______ al fútbol.
i. Cuando tenía tiempo, _________ con mi videoconsola.

3. Complete the Spanish translation in an appropriate tense.

a. *Last night I went shopping.*   Anoche, yo _______ de compras.
b. *I played on my phone.*   Yo _________ con mi móvil.
c. *Yesterday, I watched TV.*   Ayer, yo _________ la tele.
d. *I relaxed listening to music.* Yo me _______ escuchando música.
e. *I went to Javi's house.*   Yo _________ a casa de Javi.
f. *I always used to play tennis.* Yo siempre _______ al tenis.
g. *I used to go to the pool.*   Yo _________ a la piscina.
h. *I used to go out with Gemma.*   Yo_______ con Gemma.
i. *I used to watch films.*   Yo _________ películas.

4. Tangled translation (into Sp).

a. *In my* tiempo *free.*
b. *They watch* la *TV.*
c. Yo *used to read* novelas.
d. ¿Qué *you do* en tu tiempo *free*?
e. Para *to relax* yo *sing.*
f. Yo *play on* mi *mobile.*
g. Yo *always* doy un *walk.*
h. Yo *am very* activo.
i. Yo *used to dance* mucho.

5. Sentence puzzle.

a. toco instrumento No ningún   *I don't play any musical instrument.*

b. voy hace Cuando tiempo buen bicicleta en   *When the weather is nice I go cycling.*

c. Me ir compras de mis con amigos gustaba   *I used to like to go shopping with my friends.*

d. me Antes encantaba con videoconsola jugar mi   *Before, I used to love to play on my games console.*

e. Ayer vi una en la película tele bonita   *Yesterday I watched a beautiful movie on TV.*

f. pasé en ocho Instagram La horas pasada semana   *Last week I spent eight hours on Instagram.*

g. El voy fin de a ir semana cine al que viene   *Next weekend I am going to go to the cinema.*

h. tener Es importante pasatiempos   *It is important to have pastimes.*

6. Complete with the missing letters.

a. Yo pa_ _ horas en TikTok — *I spend hours on TikTok.*

b. A me_ _do hago natación — *I often go swimming.*

c. Yo voy a _ _sa de mi amiga — *I go to my friend's house.*

d. Yo j_ _ _o a video_ _egos — *I play video games.*

e. Yo _ _ _canso — *I rest.*

f. Yo _ _scar_ _ canciones — *I download songs.*

g. No h_ _ _ nada — *I don't do anything.*

h. P_ _ _ mucho tiempo… — *I spend a lot of time…*

i. …le _endo li_ _ _ _ — *…reading books.*

j. _ _ _ _ tiempo libre — *In my free time.*

7. Complete the Spanish translation.

a. Often: A me_ _ _ _

b. Rarely: _ _ _ _mente

c. Regularly: Regul_ _ _ _nte

d. Sometimes: A v_ _ _ _

e. Every day: To_ _ _ los d_ _ _

f. Last weekend: El fin de semana pa_ _ _ _

g. Next weekend: El fin de semana que v_ _ _ _

h. Never: Nu_ _ _

i. Tomorrow: _ _ña_ _

8. Complete the table.

Present	Near future	Perfect tense
	Yo voy a ir	
		Yo he jugado
Yo descargo		
	Yo voy a hacer	
		Yo he escrito
Yo leo		
	Yo voy a descansar	
		Yo he visto

9. Change verb from present to imperfect.

e.g. Yo juego al fútbol: Yo **jugaba** al fútbol.

a. Yo bailo: ___________

b. Yo hago deporte: ___________

c. Yo leo una novela: ___________

d. Yo veo una película: ___________

e. Él va a la ciudad: ___________

f. Ella va de compras: ___________

g. Ellos juegan al rugby: ___________

h. Nosotros comemos: ___________

i. Vosotros discutís: ___________

10. Translate into Spanish.

a. I go shopping: ___________

b. I go swimming: ___________

c. On my mobile: ___________

d. On my computer: ___________

e. In front of the TV: ___________

f. A new programme: ___________

g. In my free time: ___________

h. I play games: ___________

i. I go for walks: ___________

j. I rest a bit: ___________

k. I go to the cinema: ___________

l. I read a book: ___________

11. Translate into Spanish.

a. In my free time I play on my computer.

b. At the weekend I go to the shopping mall.

c. After school, I relax by listening to music.

d. On the bus, I play with my mobile phone.

e. Last night I spent two hours on the internet.

f. I love playing on my console.

g. Sometimes I read a book, but I prefer Netflix.

h. Yesterday I went to the swimming pool.

i. Last weekend I went out with my boyfriend.

j. Tomorrow I am going to watch a film at the cinema.

k. Next weekend I am going to go to Emma's party.

l. When I was little, I used to play tennis every day.

m. I used to run in the park every morning.

Unit 5 - Writing and speaking from a photo card

Write something about both of these photos in Spanish. Write about who you see, where they are and what they are doing. Read out your description.

_______________________________   _______________________________

_______________________________   _______________________________

_______________________________   _______________________________

Answer the following topic-related questions in Spanish. Read out your answers.

1. ¿Qué haces en tu tiempo libre?

____

____

2. ¿Qué hiciste el fin de semana pasado para pasar el tiempo?

____

____

3. ¿Qué vas a hacer esta tarde?

____

4. ¿Es importante tener aficiones? Justifica tu opinión.

____

____

5. ¿Qué aficiones tenías de pequeño?

____

6. ¿Qué tipo de películas y series de televisión prefieres?

____

7. ¿Te gusta leer?

____

Unit 5 - Speaking in a role-play

Look at the instructions on the left as they would appear in a speaking test. Read aloud with a partner the dialogue on the right. Then do the dialogue a second time, changing the answers or questions in bold. Take turns playing the two roles.

Foundation

<table>
<tr><td>

1. Mention a pastime you have.

2. Give one opinion about sport.

3. Ask your friend a question about pastimes.

4. Say what you do on Saturday evenings. Mention one detail.

5. Say one thing you do not like doing in your spare time.

</td><td>

1. ¿Qué haces en tu tiempo libre?
Juego al fútbol.

2. ¿Qué opinas sobre el deporte en general?
Me encanta verlo y practicarlo.

3. ¿Tienes alguna pregunta para mí?
¿Cuál es tu pasatiempo favorito?

4. ¿Qué haces los sábados por la tarde?
Veo la tele.

5. ¿Qué no te gusta hacer?
(No me gusta) montar en bicicleta.

</td></tr>
</table>

Higher

<table>
<tr><td>

1. Say what you do in your spare time (give two details).

2. Say what you think about computer games (give one opinion and one reason).

3. Ask your friend a question about free time activities.

4. Describe something you did last weekend (mention two details).

5. Say what you are going to do this evening to relax (mention one detail).

</td><td>

1. ¿Qué haces en tu tiempo libre?
Leo novelas y escucho música.

2. ¿Qué opinas sobre los videojuegos?
No me gustan porque los encuentro aburridos.

3. ¿Tienes alguna pregunta para mí?
¿Qué te gusta hacer en tu tiempo libre?

4. ¿Qué hiciste el fin de semana pasado?
Fui a un restaurante y vi una película.

5. ¿Qué vas a hacer esta tarde para relajarte?
Voy a leer un libro.

</td></tr>
</table>

Unit 5 - Foundation writing

Write approximately 50 words in Spanish. Mention all points. Refer to the language in this unit, for example the Foundation Sentence Bank, or do the task in exam conditions, without help. Or do both!

• A pastime of yours.   • When you do this.   • Computer games.   • Reading.   • What your mother likes doing.

1. ____

2. ____

3. ____

4. ____

5. ____

Using your knowledge of grammar, complete the sentences below, choosing one of the three options given.

1. Todos los días yo ______________ en bicicleta (montabas/montábamos/montaba).

2. Mi madre ______________ a menudo a la piscina (ido/ibas/va).

3. El fin de semana pasado yo ______________ al fútbol (jugué/jugaste/jugó).

4. Me encanta ______________ novelas (leo/leía/leer).

5. Vamos a dar un paseo ______________ (largos/largo/larga).

Foundation/Higher writing

Write approximately 90 words in Spanish. You must refer to each bullet point.

• Favourite pastimes.   • What you did last weekend.   • A pastime you would like to try in the future.

____

____

____

____

____

____

____

____

____

Higher writing

On paper, write approximately 150 words about free time activities. Cover both bullet points. Refer to the language in this unit, for example the Higher Sentence Bank, or do the task in exam conditions, without help. Or do both!

- The advantages and disadvantages of playing video games.
- How you recently spent time with a friend.

Unit 5 - Foundation sentence bank

Me gustan el fútbol y la música.	I like football and music.
Mi pasatiempo favorito es la lectura.	My favourite pastime is reading.
Toco la guitarra y el piano.	I play the guitar and the piano.
No toco ningún instrumento musical.	I don't play any musical instrument.
Monto en bicicleta por el campo.	I ride my bike in the countryside.
Me gusta ir de compras con mis amigos.	I like to go shopping with my friends.
Me encanta jugar con la videoconsola.	I love playing on the games console.
Anoche vi una serie en la tele.	Last night I watched a series on TV.
Me gusta salir de fiesta con mis amigos.	I like to go out partying with my friends.
El fin de semana pasado jugué al fútbol.	Last weekend I played football.
El fin de semana que viene voy a ir al cine.	Next weekend I am going to go to the cinema.
No tengo muchos pasatiempos.	I don't have many pastimes.
Tengo que salir más a menudo.	I have to go out more often.
Prefiero la natación y el hockey.	I prefer swimming and hockey.

Higher sentence bank

Es importante tener pasatiempos en la vida.	It's important to have pastimes in life.
Yo nado desde hace cinco años.	I have been swimming for five years.
Me encanta ir a la playa cuando hace buen tiempo.	I love to go to the beach when the weather is good.
Cuando era pequeña, bailaba.	When I was little, I used to dance.
El domingo que viene iré al cine.	Next Sunday I will go to the cinema.
Después de comer, fui al teatro.	After eating, I went to the theatre.
He decidido dar un paseo por el campo.	I have decided to go for a walk in the countryside.
El sábado pasado fui de compras.	Last Saturday I went shopping.
Antes jugaba a videojuegos, pero ya no me interesan.	Before, I used to play video games, but they no longer interest me.
Espero tocar un instrumento en el futuro.	I hope to play an instrument in the future.
Antes de ir a la piscina, vi a mis amigos en la ciudad.	Before going to the pool, I saw my friends in the city (or: in town).
Lo que más me gusta son las series de televisión.	What I like most are TV series.
Cuando era más joven, hacía más deporte.	When I was younger, I used to do more sport.
Reconozco que prefiero la música a la lectura.	I admit that I prefer music to reading.

ANSWERS

Unit 1 Answers
Foundation vocab building

1. Match up.

Simpático	Nice
Soltero	Single
Agradable	Pleasant
Triste	Sad
Igual	Equal
Hablador	Talkative
Divertido	Fun
Preocupado	Worried
Joven	Young
Viejo	Old

2. Broken words.
a. Novio
b. Corto
c. Niño
d. Gracioso
e. Egoísta
f. Joven
g. Viejo
h. Novia
i. Marido

3. Gapped.
a. Angry
b. Wife
c. Son, daughter
d. Worried
e. Single
f. Husband
g. Sister

4. Faulty translation.
a. Short hair
b. I get on badly
c. Happy
d. Old
e. Stepfather
f. I get angry

5. Complete the words.
a. Guapo/grande, joven, viejo.
b. Gracioso, vago, serio.
c. Padre/padrastro, madre/madrastra, novio/a, nieto/a.

6. Translate.
a. To fall
b. To get angry
c. Alone
d. Single
e. Talkative
f. To die
g. Lazy
h. To live
i. Nice
j. To spend

7. Complete.
a. Trabajador
b. Llevo
c. Hermano
d. Discuto
e. Enamora
f. Bonita
g. Matrimonio
h. Jóvenes
i. Madrastra

8. Missing letters.
a. Joven
b. Caerse
c. Vago
d. Divertido
e. Soltero
f. Vida
g. Fatal
h. Novio

9. Multiple choice.
a. Dead
b. Old
c. Nice
d. Short
e. Beautiful
f. Sad
g. Young
h. Kind
i. Alone
j. Lazy
k. Hard-working

10. Mystery word challenge.
a. Triste
b. Gracioso
c. Fatal
d. Morir
e. Discutir
f. Padres
g. Sobrina
h. Corto
i. Trabajador
j. Divorciarse

11. Break the flow.
e.g. Mi tío es alemán: *My uncle is German.*
a. Mis tíos son amables: *My uncles are kind.*
b. Mis padres son jóvenes: *My parents are young.*
c. Yo me llevo bien con mis padres: *I get on with my parents.*
d. Yo discuto con mi hermano: *I argue with my brother.*
e. Mi padre es estricto: *My father is strict.*
f. Mi hermana es trabajadora: *My sister is hard-working.*
g. Mi padre es simpático: *My father is nice.*
h Es horrible: *It's horrible.*

12. Spelling.
a. J**o**ven
b. Vie**j**o
c. Pa**d**rastro
d. Fata**l**
e. M**o**rir
f. Di**v**ertido
g. Bo**n**ito
h. **V**ago

13. Unjumble.
a. Vago
b. Joven
c. Alto
d. Bonito
e. Marido
f. Mujer
g. Amable

14. Translate into English.
a. I live with my stepmother.
b. I get on with my parents.
c. My parents understand me.
d. My sister is funny and kind.
e. My father is hard-working.
f. tMy mother is worried.
g. My little brother is sad.

Foundation reading

1. a) Fátima   b) Jaime   c) Marcos   d) Sandra   e) Cristina

2. a) Juan   b) Cecilia   c) Carlos

3. a) 5 years ago.   b) In a small flat.   c) Every weekend.   d) He works in a bakery/is mum's boyfriend/lives in his own flat /he is very kind (any two).

4. He says: a), c), d), h)

5. a) She listens to others/accepts people who are different from her/gets on well with everyone (any two).
   b) Those who don't respect everyone's differences.
   c) (i) We all have the same rights.   (ii) Doesn't like people who do not accept different identities.

6. a) Work   b) Doctors   c) Know   d) Open-minded

Unit 1 Answers
Higher vocab building

1.Match up.

Discutir	To argue
Hijo	Son
Mentir	To lie
Broma	Joke
Enfadarse	To get angry
Apoyar	To support
Cercano	Close
Caerse	To fall
Conocer	To know
Igual	Equal
Morir	To die
Hombre	Man

2. Correct.
a. Boyfriend
b Correct
c. Funny
d Correct
e. Young
f. Correct
g. Correct
h. Awful
i. Husband
j. Lazy

3. Gapped transl.
a. Get on
b. Funny
c. Daughter, son
d. Jokes
e. Mother-in-law
f. Angry
g. Separated

4. Multiple choice: circle the right option.

a. Morir	To die
b. Cuidar	To take care
c. Parecerse a	To look like
d. Trabajador	Hard-working
e. Soltero	Single
f. Vida	Life
g. Apoyar	To support
h. Joven	Young
i. Viejo	Old

7. Translate.
a. He is sad
b. I support
c. I am alone
d. He is young
e. To argue
f. To get angry
g. Single
h. Separated
i. She is nice
j. My mother-in-law
k. I like his/her face
l. She is beautiful
m. Hard-working
n. She is married
o. He is old
p. I don't mind
q. To live together
r. He is married

8. Separate the words.
a. Ella/trabaja/en/un/hospital.
b. Ella/hace/nuevos/amigos.
c. Él/se lleva/bien/con/otras/personas.
d. Yo/me/siento/sola.
e. Ellos/lo/acosan.
f. Ellos/cantan/para/pasar/el/tiempo.
g. Yo/creo/que/el/matrimonio/es/importante.
h. Mantener/una/relación/feliz.

5. Complete.
a. Paso
b. Vive
c. Simpática
d. Se parece
e. Separarse
f. Se preocupan
g. Trabajadores
h. Sola

6. Opposites.

Triste	Feliz
Vago	Trabajador
Niño	Adulto
Vivo	Muerto
Malvado	Amable
Joven	Viejo/anciano
Simpático	Antipático
Casado	Soltero
Horrible	Genial
Solo	Con pareja

9. Split sentences.

Yo paso	tiempo allí.
Mi amigo	me escucha.
Mi padre me	entiende.
Ella no está	casada.
Ellos son	amigos.
Muchos	son pobres.
Ella vive	sola.
Ellos están	divorciados.

10. Correct order.
a. Ellos no son pobres.
b. Él vive con su madre.
c. Ellos lo molestan a menudo.
d. Ella hace nuevos amigos.
e. A veces él se siente solo.
f. Ellos discuten a menudo.

11. Translate into English.
a. I often argue with my sister.
b. I live with my step-father.
c. They annoy me a lot.
d. I get on with them.
e. They do not understand me.
f. I feel alone/lonely.

12. Translate into English.
a. He has four children, two sons and two daughters.
b. She is very hard-working and ambitious.
c. They are a poor but happy family.
d. I live with my parents and my sister.
e. She does not get on with them.
f. He has been bullied by other students.
g. Fortunately, he does not feel alone and sad anymore.
h. Two years ago, he worked in a restaurant.
i. They sent their son to an orphanage.
j. They had fun singing and dancing.
k. I don't want to talk about this with my parents.
l. I have to try to stay calm all the time.
m. Her parents support her a lot.
n. I want to get married in the future.

Higher reading

1. a), d), e)
2. a) It has been quite a good day.   b) Sad/ feels alone.
   c) Why others used to react like that.
   d) They had enough problems already.
   e) Not lonely (he has friends who understand and accept him).
   f) Strong and positive.
3. c), d)
4. a) Felipe   b) Benjamín   c) Agustín   d) Martina   e) Sofía
5. a) Sensitive/responsible/happy/full of energy (any three).   b) Shared interests.   c) Reading and music.
   d) Funny/listens to her/supports her (always there for her).
6. b), c), d), f)

Unit 1 Answers
Grammar focus: adjectives

1. Complete the table.

Masculine	Feminine
Inteligente	Inteligente
Trabajador	Trabajadora
Amable	Amable
Gracioso	Graciosa
Valiente	Valiente
Moreno	Morena
Feliz	Feliz

2. Circle the correct adjective.
a. Mi padre es *divertido*.
b. Mi madre es muy *baja*.
c. Mariana está hoy muy *aburrida*.
d. Mis padres son bastante *estrictos*.
e. Mi prima es muy *trabajadora*.
f. Mis tíos son bastante *valientes*.
g. Sandra es *mentirosa*.
h. Mis tías son *simpáticas*.
i. Gianfranco es muy *musculoso*.

3. Complete the translation.
a. Mi madre es *estricta*.
b. Mi hermana es *habladora*.
c. Mi madre está *feliz*.
d. Ella parece *triste*.
e. Mis tíos son *molestos*.
f. Tu madre es *amable*.
g. Ellos son *trabajadores*.

4. Complete the translation.
a. Buen
b. Pequeño
c. Primer
d. Mal
e. Gran
f. Triste
g. Feliz
h. Valiente

5. Arrange the words in the correct order.
a. Mi padre es menos estricto que mi madre.
b. Mi hermana es más fuerte que yo.
c. Mis padres son más amables que mis tíos.
d. Nuestros primos son tan altos como nosotros.
e. Yo soy más trabajador que mi hermano.
f. Mi abuelo es tan mayor como mi abuela.

6. Tangled translation.
a. Más pequeña
b. Menos inteligente que
c. Trabajador, hermano
d. Más simpáticos.
e. Mi, más, que
f. Menos estricto, madre
g. Mi, tan, como

7. Correct.
a. Tan **buena**
b. **Gran** problema
c. ~~Más~~ inteligente
d. Más simpático**s**
e. ~~Más~~ menor
f. Más trabajador**es**
g. Son **mejores**

8. Translate.
a. A strong man.
b. A tall woman.
c. An old woman.
d. A big car.
e. A good-looking boy.
f. A new friend.
g. A beautiful house.
h. A big problem.
i. An old man.
j. A new teacher.
k. A good friend.

9. Tick and correct.

A beautiful face	*Una cara bonita*	x
A tall man	*Un hombre alto*	√
A good-looking boy	*Un chico guapo*	x
A small child	*Un niño pequeño*	x
A long road	*Una calle larga*	√
A new house	*Una casa nueva*	x
A nice person	*Una persona simpática*	√
A tall woman	*Una mujer alta*	√
A big car	*Un coche grande*	√

10. Translate.
a. Hermana
b. Padre
c. Tío
d. Hermano
e. Abuelo
f. Abuela
g. Prima
h. Tía
i. Buena
j. Alto
k. Bonita
l. Bueno
m. Grande
n. Nueva
o. Joven
p. Pequeña

11. Translate.
a. Un hombre alto.
b. Un niño pequeño.
c. Una cara bonita.
d. Una mujer mayor.
e. Un coche grande.
f. Un hombre mayor.
g. Una chica guapa.
h. Un amigo nuevo.

12. Translate into Spanish.
a. Mi madre es alta pero mi hermana es más alta que ella.
b. Mi padre es estricto y mi madre es tan estricta como él.
c. Mi abuelo tiene 73 años. Mi abuela es más joven que él.
d. Me llamo Pablo. Yo soy bajo pero mi novia es más baja que yo.
e. Mi hermano es más grande y alto que yo pero yo soy más fuerte.
f. Tengo algunos profesores buenos pero mi profesor de español es el mejor. Por supuesto.

Unit 1 Answers
Preparing for speaking and writing

1. Complete.
a. Amigo
b. Gracioso
c. Matrimonio
d. Apoyar
e. Amable
f. Alto
g. Bueno
h. Trabajador

2. Gapped translation.
a. Amable
b. Llevo
c. Más
d. Trabajador
e. Gracioso
f. Bromas
g. Joven
h. Bonita
i. Habladora

3. Broken words.
a. Bajo
b. Divertido
c. Vivo
d. Llevo
e. Es gracioso
f. Familia
g. Buen
h. Buena
i. Trabajador

4. Tangled translation.
a. Amigo, promesas
b. Apoya, tiempo
c. Mi, hay, personas
d. Mejor, se llama, gracioso
e. Cuando, con, vamos
f. Más estricta que
g. Ayer, fui, mis padres
h. Hace dos días, al cine
i. Raramente discuto

5. Anagrams.
a. Marido
b. Amigo
c. Divertido
d. Familia
e. Amable
f. Vivir
g. Pasar
h. Apoyar
i. Muerto
j. Viejo
k. Peor
l. Mejor

6. Guided translation.
a. Él es un buen amigo.
b. Mi madre es baja.
c. Mi padre es vago.
d. Yo me llevo bien con él.
e. Yo me parezco a mi madre.
f. Mi hermano es más alto.
g. Mi hermana es amable.
h. Ella me gusta mucho.
i. Él es mayor que yo.
j. Fuimos a las tiendas.
k. Yo discuto con él.
l. Mi novia es alta.

7. Complete.
a. Mi
b. Que
c. Se llama
d. Joven
e. Es
f. Con
g. Más
h. Siempre
i. Que

8. Split sentences.

En mi familia hay	cinco personas.
Un amigo ideal es	alguien amable.
Mis padres	discuten a menudo.
Mi hermano es más	inteligente que yo.
Ayer nosotros	fuimos a la piscina.
Quiero hablar de	mi tío.
Una persona a quien yo	admiro es mi padre.
Mi madre es	muy trabajadora.
Él es tan alto	como yo.
Mi hermana se	llama Fátima.

9. Correct the translations.
a. Hay **cuatro** personas.
b. Correct.
c. Ellos están **felices**.
d. Ellos comen **verduras**.
e. Hay dos **mujeres**.
f. Correct.
g. Hay tres **chicos**.
h. Ellos juegan al **fútbol**.
i. Están **tristes**.

10. Correct the spelling and grammar.
a. La mejor~~a~~ cosa.
b. Un amigo ideal.
c. Nosotros somos veganos.
d. Ella es una buena madre.
e. Hay cuatro personas.
f. Mi familia y yo.
g. Mis padres ~~se~~ discuten a menudo.
h. Mi madre es trabajadora
i. Lo **que** más me gusta de él es que es amable.

11. Translate into Spanish.
a. Me llevo bien con mis padres. Son amables.
b. A veces discuto con mis padres.
c. Creo que mi madre es amable y paciente.
d. Lo mejor de él es que me apoya.
e. Yo paso mucho tiempo con mi familia.
f. Fuimos al centro comercial. Fue divertido.
g. Mi hermana es muy simpática pero muy habladora.
h. Él es más gracioso que mi hermana pero menos trabajador.
i. Yo fui a la piscina con mi padre.

Foundation writing

1. Yo voy
2. Nosotros jugamos
3. Muy graciosa
4. Una canción nueva
5. Mis amigos salen

Unit 2 Answers
Foundation vocab building

1. Match up.

Limpio	Clean
Sucio	Dirty
Lejos	Far
Bonito	Beautiful
Joven	Young
Viejo	Old
Izquierda	Left
Derecha	Right
Calor	Hot
Frío	Cold
Pobre	Poor

2. Correct.
a. In the **countryside**.
b. It's **foggy**.
c. On the **coast**.
d. By the **sea**.
e. There is a **forest**.
f. Seven **bedrooms**.
g. There are **trees**.
h. **In front of** the house.
i. It is **cold**.

3. One of three: circle the right answer.

Verano	Summer
Lejos	Far
Invierno	Winter
Izquierda	Left
Mar	Sea
Playa	Beach
Bonito	Beautiful
Derecha	Right
Calle	Street
Sucio	Dirty

4. Tick weather words.
a. Calor √
b. Paro
c. Viento √
d. Niebla √
e. Frío √
f. Salón
g. Lluvia √
h. Mar
i. Izquierda

5. Complete.
a. Behind
b. Between
c. Fine/nice
d. Spaces
e. Clean
f. Sea

6. Translate into English.
a. Sun
b. Neighbourhood
c. Weather/time
d. Room
e. Young
f. Factory
g. To live
h. Beach
i. Rain
j. Winter
k. Sea
l. Countryside

7. Sentence puzzle.
a. Hay mucho paro.
b. En invierno hace frío y llueve muy a menudo.
c. No hay suficientes cubos de basura en las calles.
d. La vida en el campo es más tranquila y saludable.
e. En mi pueblo hay mucho ruido.
f. Mi región es bonita y está llena de lugares históricos.
g. Mi barrio es bastante tranquilo y seguro.

8. Complete.
a. Frío
b. Grande
c. Sur
d. Barrio
e. Campo
f. Lugares
g. Supermercado
h. Prefiero

9. Translate.
a. Me gustaría vivir.
b. Hay demasiados edificios.
c. Mi barrio es pobre.
d. Mi ciudad es bonita y limpia.
e. Podemos hacer deporte.
f. Doy un paseo.
g. Hace muy buen tiempo en primavera.
h. Hay menos ruido.

10. Tick.
a. Bonito
b. Contaminación √
c. Aburrido √
d. Sucio √
e. Limpio
f. Seguro
g. Horrible √
h. Violento √
i. Lluvia
j. Malo √
k. Peligroso √

11. Translate into English.

a. It's a great/big interesting city for tourists.

b. There is a small shopping centre near our home.

c. Life in the countryside is much quieter and safer.

d. Public transport is fast and cheap.

e. I like going for walks in the forest.

f. There are lots of activities for young people.

g. My neighbourhood is quite dangerous.

h. There are not many trees nor green spaces.

i. In my region the weather is good in summer and cold in winter.

j. I live in quite an old building in the city centre.

k. I prefer living in the city because life in the countryside is too quiet.

Foundation reading

1. a) Juana   b) Mario   c) Samuel   d) Juana   e) Mario   f) Samuel

2. a) Quiet   b) Forest   c) Noise   d) Nice

3. Sandra - P&N   Mateo - P   Adriana - N   Sebastián – P&N

4. Correct statements are a), c), d).

5. a) 200   b) Sing, dance (accept go to parties).   c) Swim in the sea.
   d) For boys and girls.

6. a) In a palace.
   b) Big, beautiful.
   c) Traditional houses (painted in colours), restaurants.
   d) A lot of sun.

7. 1) Old   2) Train station   3) Shopping

Unit 2 Answers
Higher vocabulary building

1. Match up.

Árbol	Tree
Río	River
Isla	Island
Campo	Countryside
Paisaje	Landscape
Calle	Street
Lugar	Place
Flor	Flower
Cerca	Near
Lejos	Far
Barrio	Neighbourhood
Costa	Coast

2. Correct.
a. To drive
d. To manufacture
e. To sell
f. To visit
h. To improve
i. To live
* Letters not included here are correct.

3. One of three: circle the right answers.

Afuera	Outside
Entre	Between
Falta	Lack
Pobre	Poor
Paisaje	Landscape
Peor	Worse
País	Country
Árbol	Tree
Cerca	Near
Costa	Coast
Sucio	Dirty

4. Spot & translate.
a. Peor
b. Detrás
c. **To eliminate**
d. **To rent**
e. Árbol
f. **To clean**
g. **To live**
h. Barrio
i. **To rain**

5. Complete.
a. Landscape
b. Sell
c. Coast
d. Clean
e. Rains
f. Quiet
g. Crosses
h. Far
i. Concern
j. Noise
k. Poor

6. Opposites.

Peor	Mejor
Comprar	Vender
Apagar	Encender
Frío	Calor
Pequeño	Grande
Ir	Volver
Sucio	Limpio
Antiguo	Nuevo
Cerrar	Abrir

7. Circle.
a. Orilla
b. Lugar
c. Paisaje
d. Cerca
e. Barrio
f. Verdes
g. Lugares
h. Árboles
i. Ruido

8. Letters.
a. Ruido
b. Árbol
c. Sucio
d. Fábrica
e. Lugar
f. Calle
g. Río
h. Lo peor
i. Falta

9. Unjumble & translate.
b. Sucio: dirty
c. Calle: street
d. Campo: countryside
e. Encender: to switch on
f. Vender: to sell
g. Comprar: to buy
h. Lugar: place

10. Break the flow.
a. Lo/peor/en/mi/ciudad/es/el/ruido/y/el/tráfico.
b. Vivo/en/el/campo,/bastante/lejos/del/centro/de/la/ciudad.
c. Por/la/noche/encienden/todas/las/luces./¡Es/precioso!
d. Por/mi/ciudad/pasa/un/río.
e. Hay/muchos/árboles/y/zonas/verdes.
f. Hay/un/festival/de/música/muy/famoso.
g. También/hay/muchos/lugares/históricos/para/visitar.
h. Lo/peor/es/que/el/transporte/público/no/es/nada/bueno.

Higher reading

1. a) West of Panama, 60 km. from Costa Rica, near Baru volcano (any two).
   b) A river and coffee plantations/2 national parks.
   c) Good weather, temperatures between 12 and 30 degrees, one of the cooler places in Panama.
   d) No, not during the flower and coffee festival.
2. 1) b 2) c 3) a 4) b
3. a) F b) P c) N d) F
4. a) Cleaner. b) Air pollution. c) Plastic waste.
   d) Use less plastic, protect forests.
5. a) Its work around sustainability.
   b) Night and day services.
   c) Can be used to move around the city.
   d) Transport on demand.
   e) Areas with fewer people.
6. 1) a 2) c 3) b 4) a
   5) Book early, tickets tend to sell out quickly.

11. Complete.
a. Vivo
b. Vende
c. Es
d. Hace
e. Hace
f. Podemos
g. Construyen
h. Deben
i. Visitar
j. Hacer
k. Va
l. Voy

12. Translate into English.
a. I like living here because people are kind and nice.
b. I have lived in Cochabamba for a few years.
c. We must improve public transport.
d. There are many historical places in our region.
e. There are many poor and homeless people.
f. After going to the cinema, we ate in a restaurant.
g. I decided to spend the day at the beach.
h. Before, I used to live in Puebla, but now I live in Cancún.
i. We must recycle in order to protect the environment.
j. I hope to live in the countryside in the future.
k. The countryside is quieter and safer than the city.
l. What I like, is that there are lots of things to do for young people.
m. I would like to live abroad for a year or two.
n. I admit that there is too much pollution and noise.
o. My region is quite poor, but the people are very kind.

Unit 2 Answers
Grammar focus: using two verbs together

1. Match up.

Poder	To be able to (can)
Querer	To want
Deber	To have to (must)
Odiar	To hate
Desear	To wish
Preferir	To prefer
Amar	To love
Esperar	To hope
Saber	To know (how to)

2. Insert.
a. Puedo
b. Debo
c. Sé
d. Gusta
e. Quiere
f. Espera
g. Prefiero
h. Gusta
i. Odio

3. Complete.
a. Vivir
b. Ver
c. Ir
d. Viajar
e. Visitar
f. Tomar
g. Gusta

4. Translate into Spanish.
a. Me gusta ir.
b. Espero vivir.
c. Quiero viajar.
d. Yo espero alquilar.
e. Ella debe ser.
f. Nosotros podemos visitar.
g. Te gusta tener.

5. Arrange the words in the correct order.
a. Yo debo ir de compras mañana por la mañana.
b. Tú puedes ir en barco por el río con amigos.
c. Hoy voy a comer en un restaurante italiano.
d. A nosotros nos gustaría vivir en el extranjero.
e. Yo espero visitar muchos monumentos aquí.

6. Tangled translation.
a. Gusta ir, con sus.
b. Quiero, castillo, campo.
c. Sabe, coche.
d. Debo reciclar, ropa.
e. Quiere vivir, capital.
f. Odiamos, pueblo.
g. Prefieres, en la ciudad, en el campo.

7. Circle and correct.
a. ~~A~~ vivir
b. Comer… alem**án**
c. Visitar
d. ~~Que~~, p**ú**blico
e. **Dar**
f. ~~A~~ visitar
g. Van **a** ir, s**á**bado

8. *A, de, que* or nothing.
a. Nothing
b. A
c. Nothing
d. A
e. Nothing
f. Que
g. Nothing
h. Nothing
i. A
j. Nothing
k. De

9. Tick and correct.

Intento ~~de~~ ayudar.
Decidí ser. ✓
Empecé **a** ver.
Me olvidé de ir. ✓
Aprendí **a** hablar.
Conseguí ~~a~~ comprar.
Acabo de **llegar**.
Acabo de comprar. ✓
Dejé **de** ir.

10. Different tenses.
a. I should live.
b. I might/could buy.
c. I would like to go.
d. I might/could live.
e. I had to go.
f. I stopped doing.
g. I will try to go.
h. I wanted to visit.

11. Translate into Spanish.
a. Intentaré visitar.
b. Me gustaría comprar.
c. Él debería quedarse.
d. Tú podrías marcharte.
e. Tuvimos que vivir.
f. Yo quería ir.
g. Me empezó/comenzó a gustar.
h. Decidí ir.

12. Translate into Spanish.
a. Me gustaría vivir en Punta Arenas pero debo comprar una casa en Buenos Aires.
b. Mi hermano desea/quiere vivir en un piso en Madrid, pero debería ir al trabajo en coche.
c. Cuando decidí visitar un castillo antiguo en el campo, mi amigo se negó a acompañarme/venir conmigo.
d. Acabo de empezar a apreciar todas las actividades en esta bonita ciudad.
e. Cuando era joven quería vivir en Madrid pero ahora quiero vivir en Barcelona.
g. Se puede vivir en la capital si se quiere disfrutar de todas las actividades posibles.

Unit 2 Answers
Preparing for speaking and writing

1. Re-arrange the words.

a. Yo vivo en un pueblo bonito al lado del mar.

b. Yo vivo en un barrio antiguo fuera de la ciudad.

c. Lo peor es el transporte público.

d. Hay muchas tiendas en el centro de la ciudad.

e. Nosotros hemos vivido aquí durante diez años.

f. Me gusta mi pueblo pero hay mucho paro.

g. Mi mayor preocupación es la contaminación del aire.

h. Yo vivo en el campo porque la vida es más tranquila.

2. Gapped translation.

a. Cubo

b. Basura

c. Lejos

d. Vivo

e. Paro

f. Mayor

g. Campo

h. Ruido

3. Tangled translation.

a. Vivo… quince…

b. Clima… región

c. Contaminación…serio

d. Barrio… peligroso

e. Peor… el crimen

f. Ha encontrado… aquí

g. Calle… tiendas

h. Casa… habitaciones

4. Translation.

a. Aquí

b. Campo

c. Ruido

d. Gente

e. Casa

f. Basura

g. Edificio

h. Calle

i. Tranquilo

j. Bonito

k. Fábricas

l. Paro

5. Complete.

a. En… en…

b. De…hay

c. Que

d. Aquí… gente…

e. Hay… mi…

f. Al… con

g. Es

h. Mucha… mi…

i. Fui… a…

j. Voy… un…

k. Basura

l. Hay…ruido…

6. Add the missing accents.

a. Mi región es bonita.

b.Tú reciclas la basura.

c. Él fue al cine.

d. Yo volví a París después de diez años.

e. Mi padre trabaja en una fábrica.

f. Me gustaría vivir en el campo.

g. Un río pasa por la ciudad.

h. Yo empecé a ir al mercado.

7. Spot and insert the missing words.

a. El año pasado **fui/viajé** a Madrid.

b. En mi casa **hay** dos baños.

c. Mi mayor preocupación **es** la contaminación.

d. El paisaje alrededor de la ciudad **es** muy bonito.

e. Mi ciudad es muy bonita **pero** hay bastante pobreza.

f. Yo nunca **reciclo** la basura.

g. **En** mi ciudad no hay tiendas.

h. Vivo bastante lejos **del** centro de la ciudad.

8. Complete with the missing vowels.

a. En mi pueblo hay muchos lugares históricos.

b. Yo vivo en una gran ciudad industrial.

c. Nosotros hemos vivido aquí cinco años.

d. La contaminación es un problema serio aquí.

e. Mi madre trabaja en el centro del pueblo.

f. Yo prefiero vivir en el campo.

g. Mi barrio es muy agradable.

9. Translate into Spanish.

a. Fábricas

b. Edificios

c. Basura

d. Campo

e. Bonito

f. Peligroso

g. Calles

h. Casas

i. Contaminado

j. Pobreza

k. Paro

l. Hay

10. Complete (accept other correct answers).

a. Vivo

b. Barrio

c. Pueblo/ciudad/barrio

d. Lugares/monumentos

e. Pueblo/apartamento

f. Bonito/agradable

g. Transporte

h. Cosas

i. Basura

j. Campo

11. Translate into Spanish.

a. He vivido en Bilbao diez años.

b. Yo vivo en un barrio antiguo en las afueras de la ciudad.

c. En mi calle hay solo dos tiendas.

d. En mi pueblo hay pocos espacios verdes.

e. Hay demasiado ruido y contaminación.

f. Demasiada gente conduce un coche.

g. Me gustaría vivir en el campo.

h. Allí, la vida es más tranquila y hay menos crimen.

i. Lo peor es que mi ciudad no es segura.

j. Algún día me gustaría vivir en el extranjero, en Francia.

k. Yo espero vivir en una gran ciudad en Italia.

Higher writing: En mi región hay muchas cosas que hacer. Sin embargo, hay demasiada contaminación en los ríos locales. La semana pasada mis amigos y yo fuimos al cine en el centro de la ciudad. El próximo domingo espero visitar un castillo en el campo con mis padres. Me gusta vivir aquí porque la gente es amable.

Unit 3 Answers
Foundation vocab building

1. Match up.

Asignatura	Subject
Futuro	Future
Curso	Course
Elección	Choice
Escuela	School
Objetivo	Goal
Carrera	Career
Dinero	Money
Trabajo	Job
Salario	Salary

2. Unscramble.
e.g. Objetivo *Goal*
a. Dinero *Money*
b. Carrera *Career*
c. Deberes *Homework*
d. Equipo *Team*
e. Lección *Lesson*
f. Asignatura *Subject*
g. Empresa *Company*
h. Inútil *Useless*
i. Explicar *To explain*

3. Gapped translation.
a. Job
b. Mistakes
c. Weak/bad
d. Subject
e. Good
f. Boring
g. Future
h. Difficult
i. School
j. Forbidden

4. Spot and correct.
a. To look for a **job**.
b. To make a **mistake**.
c. To learn a **trade**.
d. The **school day**.
e. I am **bad** at maths.
f. Correct.
g. My dream is to **travel**.
h. Correct.
i. I want to be a **scientist**.
j. Correct.

5. P/N
a. N
b. P
c. N
d. N
e. P
f. N
g. N
h. P

6. Phrase puzzle.
a. I want to become a police officer.
b. I am looking for a job.
c. My future plans.
d. I find that useless.
e. It's a hard subject.
f. I am good at Spanish.
g. I hope to earn a lot of money.

7. Complete the words and translate them.
a. Difícil: *hard*
b. Aprender: *to learn*
c. Trabajo: *job*
d. Patio: *playground*
e. Empresa: *company*
f. Útil: *useful*
g. Fácil: *easy*
h. Objetivo: *goal*
i. Habilidad: *skill*
j. Explicar: *to explain*
k. Fascinante: *fascinating*
l. Futuro: *future*
m. Profesión: *work, job*
n. Prohibir: *to prohibit*

8. Tick money words.
a. Asignatura
b. Rico ✓
c. Pobre ✓
d. Útil
e. Joven
f. Salario ✓
g. Difícil
h. Dinero ✓
i. Curso
j. Banco ✓
k. Prácticas
l. Final

9. Complete.
a. Busco
b. Asignatura
c. Rica
d. Español
e. Prácticas
f. Deberes
g. Aburrida
h. Malo

10. Translate into English.
a. Next year I will study biology.
b. I am looking for an office job.
c. My dream is to travel around the world.
d. I would like to have a well-paid job.
e. To work in the automotive/car industry.
f. I will leave school after my exams.
g. The future scares me.
h. I hate science because it's hard.
i. Next year I want to study a language.
j. I am not good at languages.

11. Translate into English.
a. I go to school on foot.
b. I think there is too much homework each/every night.
c. Last weekend I played rugby at school.
d. I don't want to go to university.
e. There are 800 students in my school.
f. Lessons start at 9 o'clock in the morning.
g. I went to the theatre with my class.
h. In the future I would like to be a lawyer.
i. School uniforms are practical.
j. I have five lessons per day.

Foundation reading

1. a) Leila   b) Jacinta   c) Leila   d) Jacinta   e) Francisco   f) Francisco
2. a) Homework   b) Playground   c) Nice
3. Sandra P/N   Mateo P   Fátima N   Juan Pablo P/N
4. Correct sentences are: a, c, f.
5. a) Languages   b) Travelling/meeting new people   c) Reading/writing stories   d) Work hard   e) Do computing/create video games
6. a) Uncomfortable   b) School trips   c) Boring   d) Weeks

Unit 3 Answers
Higher vocabulary building

1. Match up.

Entrevista	Interview
Carrera	Career
Equipo	Team
Futuro	Future
Elección	Choice
Trabajo	Job
Dinero	Money
Salario	Salary
Deberes	Homework
Empresa	Company
Enseñar	To teach
Esperar	To hope

2. Correct.
a. Confidence
b. Interview
c. Correct
d. Correct
e. To deal
f. Challenge
g. Job
h. Forbidden
i. Building

3. One of three: circle the right answers.

Objetivo	Goal
Joven	Young
Escuela	School
Trabajo	Job
Bueno	Good
A pesar de	Despite
Idioma	Language
Horrible	Horrible
Asignatura	Subject
Sueño	Dream
Útil	Useful

4. P/N
a. P
b. N
c. N
d. P
e. N
f. P
g. N
h. P
i. P

5. Complete.
a. Job
b. Chemistry
c. Bad
d. Passed
e. Young
f. Year
g. Wish/want
h. Work
i. Hope
j. Exciting
k. Bullying

6. Match the opposites.

Justo	Injusto
Bien	Mal
Horrible	Fantástico
Difícil	Fácil
Rico	Pobre
Útil	Inútil
Futuro	Pasado
Agradable	Desagradable
Vago	Trabajador

7. Translate into English.
a. To bully
b. To manage
c. Useful
d. Well-paid
e. Work, job
f. Difficult
g. To look for
h. Challenge
i. Project
j. Career
k. To dream
l. Skill
m. Success
n. Goal
o. Hope
p. Money
q. Salary
r. To allow

8. Letters.
a. Dirigir
b. Soñar
c. Práctico
d. Dinero
e. Reto
f. Joven
g. Trabajo
h. Justo
i. Bueno

9. Unjumble/translate.
e.g. Amable: *kind*
a. Buscar: *to look for*
b. Dinero: *money*
c. Útil: *useful*
d. Aprender: *to learn*
e. Equipo: *team*
f. Difícil: *hard*
g. Dirigir: *to manage*

10. Break the flow.
a. Sufrí acoso escolar cuando era pequeña.
b. Voy a tomarme un año sabático en 2030.
c. Después de los exámenes buscaré trabajo.
d. Voy a trabajar en un banco o una oficina.
e. Espero ganar mucho dinero.
f. Me gustaría trabajar en una tienda o en una escuela.
g. Me gustaría trabajar como profesor o abogado.
h. Yo sueño con ser médico en un gran hospital

11. Complete.
a. Trabajaré
b. Tomarme
c. Estudiaré
d. Sueño
e. Quiero/espero
f. Buscaré
g. Aprobar
h. Gustaría
i. Explican
j. Espero/quiero
k. Seré
l. Soy

12. Translate into English.
a. My favourite subjects are Spanish and geography.
b. I always get on with my teachers.
c. The maths teacher is strict, but kind and hard-working.
d. I think that the lessons are varied and interesting.
e. The French teacher explains the subject well.
f. I learned a lot visiting the Thyssen Museum.
g. At break I talk with my friends in the playground.
h. I want to go to university after my exams.
i. I would like to do an interesting (and) well-paid job.
j. Last night I prepared for my English exam.
k. Music is more fun than maths.
l. What I like most is seeing my best friend.
m. I would like to work abroad one day.
n. I dream of becoming a doctor.

Higher reading
1. Correct statements: a, d, f.
2. a) Scared   b) Abroad   c) A year off in England/works for a charity   d) Turn them into a job   e) Is it just a dream?
   f) Coping with everything he has to do at the moment.
3. 1) b   2) a   3) b   4) c   5) a
4. a) Looked down on.   b) Have to be twice as good, twice as qualified.   c) Is it worth the struggle?   d) Prove she is capable.
   e) Skin colour and clothes should not matter.
5. 1) b   2) a   3) c   4) a   5) b
6. a) Exciting.   b) History of planet/animal species   c) Free time to explore.   d) Never seen a museum like that.
   e) Being with friends.   f) Tired and happy.

Unit 3 Answers
Grammar focus: Simple future Tense

VERB	PRES/PAST/FUT	VERB	PRES/PAST/FUT	VERB	PRES/PAST/FUT
Preferiré	FUT	He visitado	PAST	Soy	PRES
Prefiero	PRES	Visitaré	FUT	Era	PAST
He preferido	PAST	Jugaba	PAST	Seré	FUT
Me gustó	PAST	Juego	PRES	Estudiaré	FUT
Me gusta	PRES	Jugaré	FUT	He estudiado	PAST

Normalmente voy andando al colegio.	PRES	Ayer hice mis deberes.	PAST
Ayer jugué con mis amigos.	PAST	Mañana hablaré con mis amigos.	FUT
Cuando era pequeña hablaba mucho.	PAST	El lunes pasado visité un museo.	PAST
Iré al teatro con mi clase.	FUT	Las comidas no cambian mucho.	PRES
La profesora explicó muy bien su lección.	PAST	Yo iba a la escuela primaria.	PAST
Ahora trabajo en casa.	PRES	La profesora explica bien la asignatura.	PRES
Nunca me han gustado las ciencias.	PAST	Yo me llevo bien con mis profesores.	PRES
Aprendo mucho en la clase de Música.	PRES	He trabajado dos horas. ¡Uf!	PAST
Hace dos años hacía natación.	PAST	Nosotros hablaremos mucho en clase.	FUT
El martes que viene jugaré al rugby.	FUT	Me encanta estudiar gramática.	PRES

1. Match up

Bailaré	I will dance
Hablarás	You (sing.) will talk
Escucharemos	We will listen
Bailarás	You (sing.) will dance
Hablaréis	You (plural) will talk
Escucharán	They will listen
Escucharé	I will listen
Jugaré	I will play
Iremos	We will go
Iré	I will go
Jugarás	You (sing.) will play
Iréis	You (plural) will go
Comeré	I will eat

2. Faulty translation: correct the English.

a. After school **I** will go to the park.

b. This summer **we** will go on holiday to Spain

c. My cousin**s** will go to university next year.

d. **You (plural)** will pass the physics exam if **you (plural)** study.

e. **They** will create a robot in Computer Science class.

f. In the future, **we** will need more engineers.

3. Add the missing letters

a. D**ebemos**   g. Ir**ás**   m. **Somos**

b. Ella v**a**   h. **Voy**   n. **Seremos**

c. V**eremos**   i. Ir**án**   o. **Prefiero**

d. Qu**iero**   j. L**een**   p. **Preferiré**

e. El**egirá**   k. ¿Qué h**aces?**   q. **Trabajan**

f. P**odemos**   l. **Aprenderé**   r. **Jugará**

4. Insert the right subject pronoun (yo, tú, él, etc.).

a. Nosotros/as   f. Nosotros/as   k. Nosotros/as

b. Ellos/as   g. Yo   l. Tú

c. Tú   h. Vosotros/as   m. Ellos/ellas

d. Vosotros/as   i. Él/ella   n. Nosotros/as

e. Ellos/as   j. Tú   o. Yo

                                   p. Él/ella

5. Correct the grammar mistakes.

a. ~~hablará~~ hablaré   d. ~~tú~~ vsotros estudiaréis/ tú ~~estudiaréis~~ estudiarás

b. ~~iré~~ irá   e. ~~aprobaré~~ aprobará

c. ~~iréis~~ iremos, ~~bailarás~~ bailaremos   f. ~~irá~~ irán

6. Complete with a suitable verb in the simple future tense.

a. Estudiaré

b. Iré

c. Verán

d. Jugaremos

e. Aprenderán

f. Trabajarás

g. Aprenderé

h. Estudiareis

i. Enseñará

j. Aprobaréis

Unit 3 Answers
Grammar focus: Simple future Tense - Irregular verbs

1. Match up.

Podré	I will be able to
Estudiarás	You will study
Aprobarán	They will pass
Haré	I will do
Podremos	We will be able to
Querréis	You will want
Deberemos	We will have to
Tendré	I will have
Irás	You will go
Querrá	He will want
Explicaréis	You will explain
Harán	They will do

2. Faulty translation: correct the English.

a. After school, **I will do** an apprenticeship.

b. This summer **they** will have to work.

c. Next **year**, we will study in Seville.

d. My friends **and I** will pass the English exam.

e. Where will **you** study in the future?

f. Why won't the teacher**s** teach the class?

3. Circle the correct verb conjugation.

a. Tendré

b. Estudiaremos

c. Querrá

d. Harán

e. Organizarán

f. Explicará

4. Complete the translation.

a. Yo sabré.

b. Tú podrás.

c. Nosotros organizaremos.

d. Ellos explicarán.

e. Vosotros haréis.

f. Ellos dirán.

g. Yo tendré.

h. Tú enseñarás .

i. Usted querrá.

j. Yo aprobaré.

h. Ustedes irán.

5. Circle the correct pronoun.

a. Ellos

b. Ella

c. Nosotros

d. Tú

e. Ellos

f. Tú

6. Correct the mistakes in the words in italics.

a. Ella *podrás* hacer el examen.

b. Nosotros *iremos* al gimnasio a las cuatro.

c. Mi padre *irás* a la piscina a nadar.

d. Mi hermana no *podrá* quedarse después de clase.

e. Mis hermanos *irán* a la universidad.

f. ¿A qué hora *tendrás* tú que ir a trabajar?

g. ¿*Querréis* vosotros estudiar matemáticas?

h. Yo no *sabré* responder las preguntas del examen.

7. Present, past or future? Then translate.

Ejemplo: ayer	PAST	*Yesterday*
Hoy	PRES	*Today*
Ahora	PRES	*Now*
El sábado pasado	PAST	*Last Saturday*
El sábado que viene	FUT	*Next Saturday*
Hace dos meses	PAST	*Two months ago*
Mañana	FUT	*Tomorrow*
En la actualidad	PRES	*Currently*

8. Circle the correct verb in italics.

a. Fui

b. Trabajamos

c. Jugó

d. Querrá

e. Era

f. Escucho

g. Jugaré

h. Ha encontrado

9. Complete the translation.

a. Trabajo

b. Estudiaré

c. Era

d. Trabajarán

e. Hago

f. Hizo

g. Encontraremos

10. Present to future: put these present tense verbs in the simple future tense.

e.g. Yo iré.

a. Yo trabajaré.

b. Tú serás.

c. Él tendrá.

d. Nosotros jugaremos.

e. Vosotros visitaréis.

f. Ellos saldrán.

11. Answer positively using a whole sentence. Make any changes necessary.

Students' own answers.

Unit 3 Answers
Preparing for speaking and writing

1. Complete.
a. Futuro
b. Aprobar
c. Joven
d. Trabajadora
e. Sabático
f. Convertirme
g. Tuve
h. Buscaré
i. Me/da/bien

2. Complete.
a. Buscaré
b. Trabajaré
c. Convertirme
d. Voy
e. Haré
f. Sacado

3. Complete.
a. Asignatura
b. Trabajo
c. Prácticas
d. Sueño
e. Estudiar
f. Llevo
g. Haré
h. Voy

4. Complete the table.

Masculino	Femenino
Amable	Amable
Difícil	Difícil
Trabajador	Trabajadora
Vago	Vaga
Inútil	Inútil
Bien pagado	Bien pagada
Actor	Actriz
Profesor	Profesora
Estricto	Estricta
Interesante	Interesante
Aburrido	Aburrida
Fácil	Fácil

5. Add the missing accents and translate.
a. Yo tendré un trabajo bien pagado.
   I will have a well-paid job.
b. El año que viene estudiaré español.
   Next year I will study Spanish.
c. Química es mi asignatura favorita.
   Chemistry is my favourite subject.
d. Sufrí acoso escolar de pequeña.
   I suffered bullying as a child
e. Yo prefiero las asignaturas científicas.
   I prefer scientific subjects.
f. El año que viene haré un año sabático.
   Next year I will take a sabbatical year.

6. Correct option.
a. Voy
b. Saqué
c. Terminaré
d. Busco
e. Aprobaré
f. Hago
g. Estaba
h. Seré
i. Trabajaba

7. Complete.
a. Trabajo
b. Deberes
c. Español / francés
d. Viene
e. Convertirme
f. Prácticas
g. Rico
h. Año sabático
i. Hecho

8. Sentence puzzle.
a. Yo aprendo un montón en mis clases de ciencias.
b. Yo me llevo bien con mis profesores.
c. El profesor de inglés es demasiado estricto.
d. Yo hablo con mis amigos en el patio.
e. El profesor de matemáticas explica bien la asignatura.

9. Translate into Spanish.
a. Mi asignatura favorita es español.
b. Yo me llevo bien con mis profesores.
c. El/la profesor/a de matemáticas es bastante estricto/a.
d. Yo creo que las clases son fantásticas.
e. El/la profesor/a de español explica bien la asignatura.
f. Yo aprendo un montón en mis clases de matemáticas
g. Durante el recreo hablo con mis amigos en el patio.
h. Yo sueño con ir a la universidad.
i. Yo haré un trabajo interesante y bien pagado.
j. Anoche estudié para mi examen de español.
k. La música es más divertida que las matemáticas.
l. Lo que más me gusta es ver a mis amigos.

Foundation writing

1. Voy
2. Favorita
3. Iré
4. Hablamos
5. Comenzarán

Unit 4 Answers
Foundation vocab building

1. Match up.

Lugar	Place
País	Country
Orilla	Seashore
Playa	Beach
Quedarse	To stay
Bosque	Forest
Salir	To leave
Limpio	Clean
Tiempo	Weather
Mar	Sea
Billete	Ticket

2. Correct.
a. Cold **drinks**.
b. It was **hot/warm**.
c. **Abroad**.
d. Correct.
e. **Beautiful** places.
f. Correct.
g. **Accommodation**.
h. To lose **a suitcase**.
i. Correct.

3. One of three: circle the right answer.

Maleta	*Suitcase*
Mar	*Sea*
Playa	*Beach*
Avión	*Plane*
Alquilar	*To rent*
Salir	*To leave*
Extranjero	*Foreign*
Lugares	*Places*
Comprar	*To buy*
Volar	*To fly*

4. Tick.
a. Volar √
b. Coche √
c. Autobús √
d. Tiempo
e. Playa
f. Bicicleta √
g. Avión √
h. Bosque

5. Complete.
a. Journey
b. Discover
c. Buy
d. Swim
e. Rest
f. Plane

6. Translate into English.
a. Fast/quickly
b. View
c. Weather
d. To spend time
e. Places
f. Flight
g. To stay
h. Beach
i. Hot/warm
j. Clean
k. Country
l. Foreign

7. Sentence puzzle.
a. Había playas bonitas.
b. Era bonito y hacía mucho calor.
c. Nosotros nos quedamos en un hotel bonito en la costa.
d. El vuelo a París fue corto y agradable.
e. En el pueblo había un montón de ruido.
f. La región estaba llena de lugares históricos.
h. El año pasado pasamos nuestras vacaciones en Marruecos.

8. Complete.
a. Calor
b. Bonita
c. Sur
d. Viajamos
e. Hotel
f. Lugares
g. Fantásticas
h. Prefiero

9. Translate into English.
a. I left on the 14th July.
b. I arrived on the 15th July.
c. I travelled by boat.
d. The journey was boring.
e. I stayed in a hotel on the coast.
f. I swam every day.

10. Tick all the geographical terms.
a. Montaña √
b. Cocina
c. Norte √
d. Sur √
e. Río √
f. Maleta
g. Bosque √
h. Avión
i. Región √
j. País √
k. Mar √

11. Translate into English.
a. I like to take the train and the plane, but I prefer the car.
b. Unfortunately, travelling by plane is bad for the environment.
c. I went to the beach by car with my parents.
d. You need a car in the countryside.
e. There are shops, hotels and restaurants near our campsite.
f. Last year I went to France by car and by boat.
g. Next summer I will stay in England during the holidays.
h. I like holidays by the sea because I love the beach.
i. During the holidays I bought some souvenirs for my friends.
j. I like the countryside because it is quiet and beautiful.
k. I prefer holidays abroad because they are more interesting.

Foundation reading

1. a) Francisco b) Sara c) Lisa d) Sara e) Francisco f) Lisa
2. a) Fast b) Walks c) Beach d) Plane
3. Pedro: P Adel: P/N Vega: N Montserrat: P
4. 1) c 2) a 3) b
5. a) Tourism in the Catalan Pyrenees has pros and cons. b) Tourism creates work for them.
   c) Eat in restaurants/stay in hotels and accommodations. d) Negative impact on forests.
6. 1) b 2) b 3) a
7. a) It is in the province of Pinar del Río/west of the island. b) Landscape/tobacco fields.
   c) Countryside/mountains. d) About 3 hours away by car.

Unit 4 Answers
Higher vocabulary building

1. Match up.

Costa	Coast
Mar	Sea
Lugar	Place
Vuelo	Llight
Billete	Ticket
Isla	Island
Avión	Plane
Estancia	Stay
Vista	View
Comida	Meal
Lluvia	Rain
Viento	Wind

2. Correct.

a. On the sea**shore**.
b. A foreign **country**.
c. To **go out** at night.
d. A beautiful **place**.
e. To cross the **sea**.
f. To **dream** about…
g. An **expensive** hotel.
h. A Spanish **island**.
i. A **dolphin** in the sea.

3. One of three: circle the right answers.

Fuera	Outside
Lugar	Place
Costar	To cost
Lluvia	Rain
País	Country
Estancia	Stay
Tiempo	Weather
Estrecho	Narrow
Vista	View
Vuelo	Flight
Pasar	To spend

4. Spot and translate verbs.

a. Río
b. Salir: *to go out*
c. Traducir: *to translate*
d. Extranjero
e. Sorprender: *to surprise*
f. Limpio
g. Perder: *to lose*
h. Descubrir: *to discover*

5. Complete.

a. Landscape
b. Abroad
c. Enjoyed
d. Best
e. Flight
f. Open
g. Clean
h. Chose
i. Island
j. Views
k. Stay

6. Match the opposites.

Caro	Barato
Comprar	Vender
Bueno	Malo
Frío	Calor
Salir	Llegar
Corto	Largo
Divertirse	Aburrirse
Limpio	Sucio
Perder	Encontrar

7. Circle.

a. Pasé.
b. Compré.
c. Hizo.
d. Elegí.
e. Fue.
f. Salió.
g. Perdí.
h. Compraste.
i. Fui.

8. Missing.

a. Calor
b. País
c. Hotel
d. Vista
e. Costa
f. Río
g. Corto
h. Playa
i. Comidas

9. Break the flow.

a. La isla de Cuba tiene una historia muy interesante.
b. Elegimos un hotel de lujo frente al mar en San Sebastián.
c. Pude relajarme y descansar en la playa.
d. Hizo buen tiempo casi todos los días, pero un día llovió.
e. Nos fuimos de vacaciones a las montañas de Chile.
f. Viajamos en avión y luego alquilamos un coche pequeño.
g. Lo peor fue el tiempo porque hizo frío todos los días.
h. El día fue corto pero agradable porque descansé bien.

10. Unjumble & translate.

a. Bonito	Beautiful
b. Caro	Expensive
c. Fuera	Outside
d. Mar	Sea
e. Nieve	Snow
f. Perder	To lose
g. Isla	Island

11. Complete.

a. Viajé
b. Bailé
c. Descubrí
d. Hizo
e. Elegí
f. Perdí
g. Encontré
h. Nadé
i. Compré
j. Relajé
k. Bailar
l. Debí

12. Translate into English.

a. Trains are cleaner than planes.
b. I love travelling by train because it is very fast.
c. Cycling is better for your health.
d. Despite the pollution, the car is practical.
e. Public transport is fast and on time.
f. I walked a lot when I went to Spain.
g. You can walk in the mountains.
h. I intend to stay in England this year.
i. There was a beautiful view of the sea.
j. I discovered little streets and restaurants.
k. I hope to return to France next year.
l. What I like most is the weather.
m. I would like to visit Australia one day.
n. I shall/will never forget these holidays.
o. We stayed in a hotel by the seaside.

Higher reading

1. a) 1973   b) Island's history and culture/its original inhabitants
   c) Archaeological objects/paintings/photographs
   d) 9-5 pm Monday-Friday, 9-12.30 pm Saturday.
2. a) P   b) F   c) N   d) P
3. 1) b   2) a   3) b   4) Twilight/sunset
4. a) Narrow   b) Gardens and parks
   c) Enjoy the views/take a famous photo/ visit the Crystal Palace   d) Modern and lively atmosphere
   e) Talk   f) Craftsman/artisan/tradesman
5. a) Admired landscape   b) Country house/ two floors/fields around   c) Fish/ seafood restaurants   d) After visiting a castle
   e) No rain
6. a) South Spain   b) Beach/walk in mountains   c) Go for a walk/stroll   d) Varies a lot from season to season (quite warm
   in summer, cold in winter)   e) Natural beauty/cultural wealth
7. a) 3rd floor/old apartment block/just outside San Carlos de Bariloche   b) Work will be needed   c) Small family
   d) Death of grandparents

Unit 4 Answers
Grammar focus: adverbs

1. Match up: time adverbs.

A menudo	Often
Siempre	Always
Nunca	Never
A veces	Sometimes
Tarde	Late
Bastante	Quite
Pronto	Early
Entonces	Then
Recientemente	Recently
Mañana	Tomorrow
Ayer	Yesterday
Ahora	Now
Antes	Before
Después	After

Spot the adverbs.

a. Regularmente: *regularly*

b. Ahora: *now*

c. Tarde: *late*

d. Allí: *there*

e. Aquí: *here*

f. A menudo: *often*

g. Afortunadamente: *fortunately*

h. Mucho: *a lot*

i. Bastante lejos: *quite far*

j. Muy bien: *very well*

k. Mañana: *tomorrow*

l. Tal vez: *maybe*

2. Complete.

a. Hoy

b. Siempre

c. Veces

d. Nunca

e. Después

f. Antes

g. Cerca

h. Pronto

i. Mañana

j. Tarde

k. Todavía

3. Adverbs from adjectives.

a. Actualmente

b. Rápidamente

c. Recientemente

d. Fácilmente

e. Generalmente

f. Normalmente

g. Lentamente

h. Abiertamente

i. Regularmente

j. Directamente

k. Completamente

l. Probablemente

m. Falsamente

n. Absolutamente

o. Extremadamente

p. Afortunadamente

q. Ciertamente

r. Finalmente

4. Translate into English.

a. Well

b. Better

c. Badly

d. Worse

e. Still, again

f. Already

g. Even

h. After

i. Nearby/Close

5. Add the missing letters.

a. Lentamente

b. Fácilmente

c. Siempre

d. A veces

e. Ahora

f. Antes

g. Hoy

h. Ayer

i. Incluso

j. Recientemente

k. A menudo

l. Pronto

m. Muy

n. Nunca

o. Cerca

p. Mañana

q. Deprisa

r. Mejor

6. Add the vowels.

a. Generalmente — *Generally*

b. Absolutamente — *Absolutely*

c. Relativamente — *Relatively*

d. Extremadamente — *Extremely*

e. Realmente — *Really*

f. Actualmente — *Currently*

g. Perfectamente — *Perfectly*

h. Afortunadamente — *Fortunately*

i. Ciertamente — *Certainly*

7. Translate.

a. Ayer

b. Mañana

c. A veces

d. Después

e. Ahora

f. Antes

g. Ya

h. Ahí/allí

i. Aquí/acá

j. Entonces

k. Siempre

l. Mejor

m. Peor

n. Rápidamente

o. Recientemente

8. How, where, when.

a. Mañana

b. Bien

c. Allí

d. Tranquilamente

e. Pronto

f. Lejos

g. Mucho

h. Bien

i. Bastante

9. Translate into Spanish (easier).

a. Yo vuelo un montón/mucho.

b. Viajo a Londres a menudo.

c. Nosotros nunca vamos a España.

d. Ya he comprado un billete.

e. A veces voy al trabajo a pie.

f. Ayer visité el mercado.

g. Recientemente ella fue a Chile en avión.

10. Translate into Spanish (harder).

a. En verano nosotros viajamos a menudo a España en coche.

b. Yo iré a Escocia pronto.

c. Después de visitar Buenos Aires, fuimos a Rosario en tren.

d. A veces prefiero llegar pronto a mi destino.

e. ¿Ya has visitado Suiza en tren?

f. Realmente queremos ir a Francia el año que viene.

g. Puedo viajar directamente a mi destino en coche.

h. Afortunadamente, hizo buen tiempo en Bolivia el año pasado.

i. Yo no viajo nunca al extranjero en avión.

j. ¿Tú vuelas regularmente a Londres o vas en coche?

k. A nosotros siempre nos gusta visitar países nuevos.

l. Reservaré los billetes en línea antes de ir a Montreal.

m. Nosotros nos quedamos a menudo en Inglaterra, incluso si hace mal tiempo.

n. El año que viene probablemente no iré de vacaciones.

Unit 4 Answers
Preparing for speaking and writing

1. Split sentences.

El hotel era	muy bonito pero caro.
Estoy de	vacaciones junto al mar.
Voy a	montar en bicicleta.
Prefiero	volar a viajar en tren.
El verano pasado	fui a Canadá.
Normalmente	voy al aeropuerto en taxi.
Casi nunca voy al	extranjero.
Me gusta descubrir	nuevos países.
Mi sueño es	vivir en otros países.

2. Broken words.
a. Vacaciones
b. Medios
c. Descubrir
d. Campo
e. Alojamiento
f. Alquilar… coche
g. Pasar… semana
h. Perder… maleta
i. Probar
j. Orilla… mar

3. Complete.
a. Año… Colombia
b. Viajé… alquilé
c. Elegimos… mar
d. Mañana… playa
e. Nadé… leí
f. Relajé
g. Salí… bailé
h. Probé… local
i. Sueño… ir

4. Tangled translation.
a. Yo fui
b. Al extranjero
c. En barco
d. El río
e. Alojamiento
f. Elegir
g. Vistas
h. Históricos
i. Pasar
j. Relajé
k. Visité

5. Complete the answers to the questions.
a. ¿Adónde fuiste de vacaciones el año pasado?
b. *Fui a Marruecos con mi **familia**.*

a. ¿Cómo viajaste?
b. *Viajé en **avión**.*

a. ¿Dónde te alojaste?
b. *Me **alojé** en un hotel enfrente del **mar**.*

a. ¿Cómo fue el viaje?
b. *Fue **muy** bien pero demasiado **caro**.*

a. ¿Qué hiciste?
b. ***Nadé** en el mar y **leí** un libro.*

a. ¿Qué cosas interesantes viste?
b. *Vi muchos animales y varios **lugares** históricos.*

6. Complete (accept other suitable verbs).
a. Viajé
b. Compré
c. Visité/vi/fui a
d. Probé/comí
e. Pasé/estuve
f. Relajé
g. Di
h. Alquilé
i. Tomé
j. Llegué

7. Sentence puzzle.
a. Yo fui de vacaciones a Marruecos.
b. Me alojé en un hotel caro.
c. Me encanta visitar lugares históricos.
d. Prefiero ir a la montaña.
e. Pasé dos semanas en la República Dominicana.
f. Me encanta ir a países extranjeros

8. Correct the mistakes.
a. Me alojé
b. Yo he viajado
c. Fui
d. A la escuela
e. Yo salí
f. Me relajé
g. Año, iré
h. La comida

9. Add the missing accents.
a. Fui a la playa en autob**ú**s.
b. Me encanta visitar pa**í**ses extranjeros.
c. Voy todos los d**í**as a la escuela en coche.
d. Me aloj**é** en un hotel cerca de la playa.
e. Descans**é** mucho tiempo en la playa.
f. Escuch**é** m**ú**sica en el coche.
g. Prefiero los lugares hist**ó**ricos.
h. He hablado franc**é**s durante las vacaciones.

10. Translate into Spanish.
a. A menudo me gusta tomar el tren y el avión
b. Prefiero el tren porque es rápido y limpio.
c. El avión es malo para el medio ambiente.
d. Ayer fui a la playa en coche.
e. Normalmente voy a la escuela a pie.
f. Afortunadamente no necesitamos un coche.
g. Cerca de mi casa hay tiendas y hoteles.
h. Había una vista fantástica del mar.
i. Descubrí calles pequeñas y comí comida deliciosa.
j. Espero volver a Perú el año que viene.

Foundation writing

1. Quedaremos
2. Toma
3. Visité
4. Antiguo
5. Viajar

Unit 5 Answers
Foundation vocab building

1. Match up.

Nadar	To swim
Jugar	To play
Leer	To read
Correr	To run
Aprender	To learn
Descargar	To download
Perder	To lose
Hacer	To do
Ver	To watch
Escuchar	To listen
Bailar	To dance

2. Correct.
a. I love to **sing**.
b. I would like to **read**.
c I used to like to **run**.
d. I like to **play**.
e. I hate to **learn**.
f. Correct.
g. Correct.
h. I often **swim**.

3. One of three: circle the right answer.

Ver	To watch
Escribir	To write
Bicicleta	Bike
Emocionante	Exciting
A veces	Sometimes
Portátil	Laptop
Novela	Novel
Perder	To lose
Estadio	Stadium
Ganar	To win

4. Tech words.
a. Portátil √
b. Natación
c. Descargar √
d. Ordenador √
e. Estadio
f. En línea √
g. Paseo
h. Pantalla √

5. Complete.
a. Programme
b. Bicycle
c. Download
d. Novel
e. Chatting online
f. Go out

6. Translate into English.

Spanish	English	Spanish	English
Siempre	Always	Perder	To lose
A menudo	Often	Pasar	To spend time
A veces	Sometimes	Descargar	To download
Nunca	Never	Interesarse	To be interested

7. Sentence puzzle.
a. Juego en mi móvil todos los días.
b. No hago mucho deporte.
c. Yo paso dos horas al día en internet.
d. Me gusta dar un paseo en el parque.
e. A menudo salgo con mi novio después del colegio.
f. Mi pasatiempo favorito es montar en bicicleta.
g. Veo películas y programas de música.

8. Complete.
a. Veo
b. Montaré
c. Juego
d. Paso
e. Hablé
f. Salí
g. Iré
h. Leo

9. Translate.
a. I went to the stadium.
b. I spend an hour on Youtube.
c. I did sport.
d. I will watch a TV programme.
e. Before/Previously, I always used to listen to K-Pop.
f. I would go out with my friends.

10. Negatives.
a. Bonito
b. Simpático
c. Aburrido √
d. Horrible √
e. Gracioso
f. Incorrecto √
g. Peligroso √
h. Perder √
i. Pésimo √
j. Malo √
k. Bien

11. Translate into English.
a. I like football and music. My favourite music is hip hop.
b. I love to read/reading. My favourite novels are crime/detective novels.
c. I play the guitar and the piano. Also, I like to draw.
d. I don't play a musical instrument, but I would like to learn.
e. When the weather is nice, I ride my bicycle in the countryside.
f. I would like to go shopping with my friends.
g. I love playing videogames with friends.
h. Yesterday afternoon/evening I watched a series on TV. It was great!
i. I like partying with my friends. I love to dance!
j. Last weekend I played on my computer for ten hours!
k. Next weekend I will go to my friend Martina's (house).

Foundation reading

1. a) Carla   b) Antonio   c) Víctor   d) Carla   e) Víctor   f) Antonio
2. a) Badly   b) Garden   c) Ice creams
3. Amanda P   Mohamed P/N   Gustavo N   Helena N
4. 1) c   2) a   3) b   4) b   5) c   6. If you are in the sea it is less dangerous if you know how to swim.
5. a) Everywhere.   b) More than a hobby, it's a way of life.   c) Play in a top team.   d) Play too/but less often.
6. a) Writes songs.   b) Because it is difficult.   c) Wrote a song about a character in a novel.   d) Play in a band.
7. Football P   Swimming P   Cycling N   Running F

Unit 5 Answers
Higher vocabulary building

1. Match up.

Pantalla	Screen
Ordenador	Computer
Libro	Book
Móvil	Mobile
Videojuego	Videogame
Juego	Game
Lectura	Reading
En línea	Online
Novela	Novel
Compras	Shopping
Interés	Interest
Canción	Song

2. Correct.

a. Correct
b. To **learn**
c. To **win, earn**
d. Correct
e. To **read**
f. To **write**
g. To **go out**
h. To **download**

3. One of three: circle the right answers.

Gusto	Taste
Equipo	Team
Correr	To run
Probar	To try
Juego	Game
Novela	Novel
Perder	To lose
La cancha	Pitch
Leer	To read
Pasar	To spend

4. Tick.

a. Escuchar
b. Pasear √
c. Leer
d. Nadar √
e. Correr √
f. Ver
g. Descansar
h. Bailar √
i. Montar en bici √

5. Complete.

a. Series
b. Nothing
c. Rested
d. Novels
e. Football pitch
f. Swimming
g. Sometimes
h. Spend
i. Games
j. Mobile phone

6. Match the opposites.

Perder	Ganar
Siempre	Nunca
Aburrido	Divertido
Descansar	Cansarse
Horrible	Genial
Sano	Malsano
Demasiado	Poco
Salir	Quedarse
Caro	Barato

7. Circle.

a. Compras
b. Veo
c. Perdí
d. Interesan
e. Escuchaba
f. Paso
g. Intento
h. Voy
i. Leer

8. Letters.

a. Perder
b. Novela
c. Correr
d. Pasar
e. Descansar
f. Ganar
g. Campo
h. Caro
i. Intentar

9. Unjumble.

e.g. Libro	Book
a. Perder	To lose
b. Ganar	To win, earn
c. Interés	Interest
d. Salir	To go out
e. Intentar	To try
f. Leer	To read
g. Gusto	Taste

10. Break the flow. Insert lines where there should be gaps.

a. En mi opinión es importante tener aficiones en la vida.
b. Nado en la piscina desde hace cinco años.
c. Me encanta ir a la playa cuando hace calor.
d. Cuando era pequeña bailaba dos veces a la semana.
e. He decidido dar un paseo en el campo.
f. El sábado pasado fui de compras con mis amigos.
g. Antes jugaba a videojuegos pero ya no me interesan.

11. Complete.

a. Leía	e. Escuché	i. Paso
b. Aprendí	f. Voy	j. Quedar
c. Iré	g. Encantan	k. Pasado
d. Gustaría	h. Relajo	l. Veo

12. Translate into English.

a. It's important to have pastimes in life.
b. I have been swimming for five years.
c. I love going to the beach when the weather is good.
d. When I was little, I used to dance (or: I tended to dance).
e. Next Sunday we're going to go to the cinema.
f. After eating, I went to the theatre.
g. I have decided to go for a walk in the countryside.
h. Last Saturday I went shopping.
i. Before, I used to play video games…
j. … but they no longer interest me.
k. I hope to be able to play an instrument in the future.
l. Before going to the pool, I saw my friends in town (or: in the city).
m. What I like most are TV series.
n. When I was younger, I used to do more sport.
o. I admit that I prefer music to reading.
p. I spend an hour or two per day on Youtube.

Higher reading

1. 1) a   2) b   3) Ride a bike/walking/enjoying the sun   4) The latest ones   5) a
2. a) F   b) P   c) N   d) N
3. a) Perform music in public.   b) They thought her education was more important.   c) Finished university.
   d) Sang in front of 100 people at a wedding.   e) She will release songs online.
4. a) Be stronger/weigh less/be healthy.   b) Running/swimming/cycling/dance.   c) Relax/meet new people.
   d) Most popular/ majority of Uruguayan people listen to music every day.
   e) The number of downloads of national videogames exceeded 10 million.
5. a) Shopping.   b) Tried on clothes/ had fun.   c) A bit boring.   d) Watched a film with family.   e) Read a new novel.
6. a) Fixed his motorbike. b) Good to relax/have fun. c) Went to the library/to study/ read a book about history of Honduras.
   d) He's crazy. e) Never made it before. f) Might open a restaurant some day.
7. 1) c   2) c   3) a

Unit 5 Answers
Grammar focus: Imperfect Tense

Solía jugar al fútbol con mis amigas.	IMP
Me gusta ir al cine los fines de semana.	PRES
Ahora tengo muchas aficiones.	PRES
He ido a nadar con dos amigas mías.	PERF
Yo paseaba a menudo por la ciudad con mi novio.	IMP
Había una piscina no muy lejos de la estación de tren.	IMP
Hay un polideportivo cerca de mi casa.	PRES
He visto a mi amiga Celia en la cafetería.	PERF
Siempre veo a mis amigos en el centro comercial.	PRES
Hago danza y yoga.	PRES
Hacía más deporte cuando era más joven.	IMP
He salido a pasear por la playa con mi novia.	PERF
Normalmente monto en bici cuando hace buen tiempo.	PRES
Me gustaba ir en bici por el campo.	IMP

1. Match up.

Nosotras	veíamos el partido.
Tú	nadabas en la piscina.
Yo/Marc	iba en bicicleta.
Yo/Marc	jugaba al fútbol.
Vosotros	jugabais al ajedrez.
Ellas	bailaban.

2. Best verb.
a. Caminaba
b. Gustaba
c. Venía
d. Hacía
e. Corrían
f. Encantaba
g. Comías

3. Present to imperfect.
a. Yo iba al cine.
b. Yo jugaba al fútbol.
c. Yo montaba en bici.
d. Yo salía con mis amigos.
e. Yo era muy deportista.
f. Yo tenía muchos amigos.
g. Me gustaba la música.
h. Me encantaba leer.

4. Complete.
a. Jugaba
b. Bailaba
c. Pasábamos
d. Leíais
e. Escribía
f. Escuchabas
g. Iba
h. Era (x2)

5. Question and answers (possible answers).
a. No, iba a la piscina.
b. No, veía dibujos animados.
c. No, yo era vago/a.
d. Sí, tenía muchos amigos.
e. No, me quedaba en casa/descansaba.
f. No, odiaba leer / Sí, me gustaba mucho.
g. No, no tenía muchos/tantos deberes.
h. Sí, jugaba todos los días / No, me encantaba leer.
i. No, yo bebía agua/leche/refrescos, etc.

6. Insert the missing vowels.
a. Yo comía dulces.
b. Nosotros jugábamos a las cartas.
c. Ellos/as daban muchos paseos.
d. Ella iba a la discoteca.
e. ¿Ibais al estadio de pequeños?
f. Yo veía series de televisión.
g. Usted leía novelas.
h. Tú jugabas en el parque.
i. Yo era más deportista.

7. Choose.
a. Leía
b. Tenías
c. Jugaba
d. Íbamos
e. Ibais
f. Era
g. Era
h. Encantaba

8. Translate into Spanish.
a. Yo jugaba al fútbol con mis amigos.
b. Yo era más deportista que ahora.
c. Nosotros íbamos al cine mucho.
d. ¿Qué hacías/estabas haciendo ayer?
e. Yo hablaba/estaba hablando con mis amigos en clase.

9. What did you do on weekdays as a child?
a. A las ocho de la mañana, yo iba al colegio/a la escuela.
b. A las diez, yo trabajaba en clase.
c. A las once, yo hablaba con mis amigos/as.
d. A las doce, yo hablaba español.
e. A las doce y media, yo comía en el colegio/la escuela.
f. A las tres y media, yo volvía a casa.
g. A las seis, yo hacía los deberes.
h. A las siete, yo mandaba un mensaje a un/a amigo/a.
i. A las ocho, yo veía una serie.
j. A las nueve, yo escuchaba música.
k. A las nueve y media, yo bebía un poco de leche.
l. A las diez, yo me iba a la cama.

Unit 5 Answers
Preparing for speaking and writing

1. Missing letters.
a. Leeré…novela
b. Jugué…móvil
c. Veo…serie
d. Relajo…habitación
e. Salgo…amigo
f. Jugaba…fútbol
g. Escucharé…música
h. Iría…centro comercial
i. Corrí
j. Chateo…mis amigos

2. Complete.
a. Iba
b. Hacía
c. Iba
d. Iba
e. Jugaba
f. Era
g. Hacía
h. Jugaba
i. Jugaba

3. Complete.
a. Fui
b. Jugué
c. Vi
d. Relajé
e. Fui
f. Jugaba
g. Iba
h. Salía
i. Veía

4. Tangled translation.
a. En mi…libre
b. Ellos/ellas ven… televisión
c. Leía
d. Haces / libre
e. Relajarme…canto
f. Juego…en…móvil
g. Siempre / paseo
h. Soy muy
i. Bailaba

5. Sentence puzzle.
a. No toco ningún instrumento.
b. Cuando hace buen tiempo voy en bicicleta.
c. Me gustaba ir de compras con mis amigos.
d. Antes me encantaba jugar con mi videoconsola.
e. Ayer vi una película bonita en la tele.
f. La semana pasada pasé ocho horas en Instagram.
g. El fin de semana que viene voy a ir al cine.
h. Es importante tener pasatiempos.

6. Complete.
a. Paso
b. Menudo
c. Casa
d. Juego…videojuegos
e. Descanso
f. Descargo
g. Hago
h. Paso
i. Leyendo…libros
j. En…mi

7. Complete.
a. A menudo
b. Raramente
c. Regularmente
d. A veces
e. Todos los días
f. Pasado
g. Que viene
h. Nunca
i. Mañana

8. Complete the table.

Present	Near future	Perfect tense
Yo voy	Yo voy a ir	Yo he ido
Yo juego	Yo voy a jugar	Yo he jugado
Yo descargo	Yo voy a descargar	Yo he descargado
Yo hago	Yo voy a hacer	Yo he hecho
Yo escribo	Yo voy a escribir	Yo he escrito
Yo leo	Yo voy a leer	Yo he leído
Yo descanso	Yo voy a descansar	Yo he descansado
Yo veo	Yo voy a ver	Yo he visto

9. Present to imperfect.
e.g. Yo jugaba al fútbol.
a. Yo bailaba.
b. Yo hacía deporte.
c. Yo leía una novela.
d. Yo veía una película.
e. Él iba a la ciudad.
f. Ella iba de compras.
g. Ellos jugaban al rugby.
h. Nosotros comíamos.
i. Vosotros discutíais.

10. Translate into Spanish.
a. Yo voy de compras.
b. Yo nado/hago natación.
c. En mi móvil.
d. En mi ordenador.
e. Delante de la tele.
f. Un programa nuevo.
g. En mi tiempo libre.
h. Yo juego a juegos.
i. Yo doy paseos.
j. Yo descanso un poco.
k. Yo voy al cine.
l. Yo leo un libro.

11. Translate into Spanish.
a. En mi tiempo libre yo juego con el/mi ordenador.
b. El fin de semana yo voy al centro comercial.
c. Después del colegio/de la escuela, me relajo escuchando música.
d. En el autobús, yo juego con mi móvil.
e. Anoche pasé dos horas en internet.
f. Me encanta jugar con mi videoconsola.
g. A veces leo un libro pero prefiero Netflix.
h. Ayer fui a la piscina.
i. El fin de semana pasado salí con mi novio.
j. Mañana voy a ver una película en el cine.
k. El fin de semana que viene voy a ir a la fiesta de Emma.
l. Cuando era pequeño/a, yo jugaba al tenis todos los días.
m. Yo corría por el parque todas las mañanas.

Foundation writing
1. Montaba   2. Va   3. Jugué   4. Leer   5. Largo